Bhagavad Gita

Bhagavad Gita

translated by Swami Swarupananda

Being a Discourse Between Arjuna,
Prince of India, and the Supreme Being
Under the Form of Krishna

Table of Contents

The Grief of Arjuna

Dhritarashtra said:

1) Tell me, O Sanjaya! Assembled on Kurukshetra, the center of religious activity, desirous to fight, what indeed did my people and the Pandavas do?

Sanjaya said:

2) But then King Duryodhana, having seen the Pandava forces in battle array, approached his teacher Drona and spoke these words:

3) "Behold, O Teacher! this mighty army of the sons of Pandu, arrayed by the son of Drupada, your gifted pupil.

4-6) "Here [are] heroes, mighty archers, the equals in battle of Bhima and Arjuna-the great warriors Yuyudhana, Virata, Drupada; the valiant Dhrishtaketu, Chekitana, and the king of Kashi; the best of men, Purujit, Kuntibhoja, and Shaibya; the powerful Yudhamanyu, and the brave Uttamaujas, the son of Subhadra and the sons of Draupadi-all of whom are lords of great chariots.

7) "Hear also, O best of the twice-born! the names of those who [are] distinguished amongst ourselves, the leaders of my army. These I relate [to you] for your information.

8) "Yourself and Bhishma and Karna and Kripa, the victorious in war. Ashvatthama and Vikarna and Jayadratha, the son of Somadatta.

9) "And many other heroes also, well-skilled in fight, and armed with many kinds of weapons, are here, determined to lay down their lives for my sake.

10) "This our army defended by Bhishma [is] impossible to be counted, but that army of theirs, defended by Bhima [is] easy to number.

11) "[Now] do, being stationed in your proper places in the divisions of the army, support Bhishma alone."

12) That powerful, oldest of the Kurus, Bhishma the grandsire, in order to cheer Duryodhana, now sounded aloud a lion-roar and blew his conch.

13) Then following Bhishma, conchs and kettle-drums, tabors, trumpets, and cowhorns blared forth suddenly from the Kaurava side, and the noise was tremendous.

14) Then, also, Madhava and Pandava, stations in their magnificent Chariot yoked with white horses, blew their divine conchs with a furious noise.

15) Hrishikesha blew the Panchajanya, Dhananjaya, the Devadatta,and Vrikodara, the doer of terrific deeds, his large conch Paundra.

16) King Yudhishthira, son of Kunti, blew the conch named Anantavijaya, and Nakula and Sahadeva, their Sughosha and Manipushpaka.

17) The expert bowman, king of Kashi, and the great warrior Shikhandi, Dhristadyumna, and Virata, and the unconquered Satyaki;

18) O Lord of Earth! Drupada and the sons of Draupadi, and the mighty-armed son of Subhadra, all, also blew each his own conch.

19) And the terrific noise resounding throughout heaven and earth rent the hearts of Dhritarashtra's party.

20) Then, O Lord of Earth, seeing Dhritarashtra's party standing marshalled and the shooting about to begin, the Pandava, whose ensign was the monkey, raising his bow, said the following words to Krishna:

Arjuna said:

21-22) Place my chariot, O Achyuta! between the two armies that I may see those who stand here prepared for war. On this eve of battle [let me know] with whom I have to fight.

23) For I desire to observe those who are assembled here for fight, wishing to please the evil-minded Duryodhana by taking his side on this battle-field.

Sanjaya said:

24-25) O Bharata, commanded thus by Gudakesha, Hrishikesha drove that grandest of chariots to a place between the two hosts, facing Bhishma, Drona, and all the rulers of the earth, and then spoke thus, "Behold, O Partha, all the Kurus gathered together!"

26) Then saw Partha stationed there in both the armies, grandfathers, fathersin- law, and uncles, brothers and cousins, his own and their sons and grandsons, and comrades, teachers, and other friends as well.

27) Then, he, the son of Kunti, seeing all those kinsmen stationed in their ranks, spoke thus sorrowfully, filled with deep compassion.

Arjuna said:

28-29) Seeing, O Krishna, these my kinsmen gathered here eager for fight, my limbs fail me, and my mouth is parched up. I shiver all over, and my hair stands on end. The bow Gandiva slips from my hand, and my skin burns.

30) Neither, O Keshava, can I stand upright. My mind is in a whirl. And I see adverse omens.

31) Neither, O Krishna, do I see any good in killing these my own people in battle. I desire neither victory nor empire, nor yet pleasure.

32-34) Of what avail is dominion to us, of what avail are pleasures and even life, if these, O Govinda! for whose sake it is desired that empire, enjoyment, and pleasure should be ours, themselves stand here in battle, having renounced life and wealth–teachers, uncles, sons, and also grandfathers, maternal uncles, fathers-in-law, grandsons, brothers-in-law, besides other kinsmen.

35) Even tough these were to kill me, O slayer of Madhu, I could not wish to kill them–not even for the sake of dominion over the three worlds, how much less for the sake of the earth!

36) What pleasure indeed could be ours, O Janardana, from killing these sons of Dhritarashtra? Sin only could take hold of us by the slaying of these felons.

37) Therefore we ought not to kill our kindred, the sons of Dhritarashtra. For how could we, O Madhava, gain happiness by the slaying of our own kinsmen?

38-39) Though these, with understanding overpowered by greed, see no evil due to decay of families, and no sin in hostility to friends, why should we O Janaradana, who see clearly the evil due to the decay of families, not turn away from this sin?

40) On the decay of a family the immemorial religious rites of that family die out. On the destruction of spirituality, impiety further overwhelms the whole of the family.

41) On the prevalence of impiety, O Krishna, the women of the family become corrupt; and women being corrupted, there arises, O Varshneya, intermingling of castes.

42) Admixture of castes, indeed is for the hell of the family and the destroyers of the family; their ancestors fall, deprived of the offerings of rice-ball and water.

43) By these misdeeds of the destroyers of the family, bringing about confusion of castes, are the immemorial religious rites of the caste and the family destroyed.

44) We have heard, O Janardana, that dwelling in hell is inevitable for those men in whose families religious practices have been destroyed.

45) Alas, we are involved in a great sin, in that we are prepared to slay our kinsmen, out of greed for the pleasures of a kingdom!

46) Verily, if the sons of Dhritarashtra, weapons in hand, were to slay me, unresisting and unarmed, in the battle, that would be better for me.

Sanjaya said:
47) Speaking thus in the midst of the battle-field, Arjuna, casting away his bow and arrows, sank down on the seat of his chariot, with his mind distressed with sorrow.

The Way of Knowledge

Sanjaya said:

1) To him who was thus overwhelmed with pity and sorrowing, and whose eyes were dimmed with tears, Madhusudana spoke these words.

The Blessed Lord said:

2) In such a crisis, whence comes upon you, O Arjuna, this dejection, un-Arya-like, disgraceful, and contrary to the attainment of heaven?

3) Yield not to unmanliness, O son of Pritha! Ill does it become you. Cast off this mean faintheartedness and arise, O scorcher of your enemies!

Arjuna said:

4) But how can I, in battle, O slayer of Madhu, fight with arrows against Bhishma and Drona, who are rather worthy to be worshipped, O destroyer of foes!

5) Surely it would be better even to eat the bread of beggary in this life than to slay these great-souled masters. But if I kill them, even in this world, all my enjoyment of wealth and desires will be stained with blood.

6) And indeed I can scarcely tell which will be better, that we should conquer them, or that they should conquer us. The very sons of Dhritarashtra-after slaying whom we should not care to live-stand facing us.

7) With my nature overpowered by weak commiseration, with a mind in confusion about duty, I supplicate You. Say decided what is good for me. I am Your disciple. Instruct me who have taken refuge in You.

8) I do not see anything to remove this sorrow which blasts my senses, even were I to obtain unrivalled and flourishing dominion over the earth, and mastery over the gods.

Sanjaya said:

9) Having spoken thus to the Lord of the senses, Gudakesha, the scorcher of foes, said to Govinda, "I shall not fight," and became silent.

10) To him who was sorrowing in the midst of the two armies, Hrishikesha, as if smiling, O descendant of Bharata, spoke these words.

The Blessed Lord said:

11) You have been mourning for them who should not be mourned for. Yet you speak words of wisdom. The [truly] wise grieve neither for the living nor for the dead.

12) It is not that I have never existed, nor you, nor these kings. Nor is it that we shall cease to exist in the future.

13) As are childhood, youth, and old age, in this body, to the embodied soul, so also is the attaining of another body. Calm souls are not deluded thereat.

14) Notions of heat and cold, of pain and pleasure, are born, O son of Kunti, only of the contact of the senses with their objects. They have a beginning and an end. They are impermanent in their nature. Bear them patiently, O descendant of Bharata.

15) That calm man who is the same in pain and pleasure, whom these cannot disturb, alone is able, O great amongst men, to attain to immortality.

16) The unreal never is. The real never is not. Men possessed of the knowledge of the Truth fully know both these.

17) That by which all this is pervaded–That know for certain to be indestructible. None has the power to destroy this Immutable.

18) Of this indwelling self–the ever-changeless, the indestructible, the illimitable–these bodies are said to have an end. Fight, therefore, O descendant of Bharata.

19) He who takes the self to be the slayer, and he who takes it to be the slain, neither of these knows. It does not slay, nor is it slain.

20) This is never born, nor does it die. It is not that, not having been, it again comes into being. [Or according to another view: It is not that having been, it again ceases to be.] This is unborn, eternal, changeless, ever-itself. It is not killed when the body is killed.

21) He that knows this to be indestructible, changeless, without birth, and immutable, how is he, O son of Pritha, to slay or cause another to slay?

22) Even as a man casts off worn-out clothes, and puts on others which are new, so the embodied casts off worn-out bodies, and enters into others which are new.

23) This [self], weapons cut not; this, fire burns not; this, water wets not; and this, wind dries not.

24) This self cannot be cut, nor burnt, nor wetted, nor dried. Changeless, all-pervading, unmoving, immovable, the self is eternal.

25) This [self] is said to be unmanifested, unthinkable, and unchangeable. Therefore, knowing this to be such, you ought not to mourn.

26) But if you should take this to have constant birth and death, even in that case, O mighty-armed, you ought not to mourn for this.

27) Of that which is born, death is certain; of that which is dead, birth is certain. Over the unavoidable, therefore, you ought not to grieve.

28) All beings are unmanifested in their beginning, O Bharata, manifested in their middle state, and unmanifested again in their end. What is there then to grieve about?

29) Some look upon the self as marvelous. Others speak of it as wonderful. Others again hear of it as a wonder. And still others, though hearing, do not understand it at all.

30) This, the indweller in the bodies of all, is ever indestructible, O descendant of Bharata. Therefore you ought not to mourn for any creature.

31) Looking at your own dharma, also, you ought not to waver, for there is nothing higher for a kshatriya than a righteous war.

32) Fortunate certainly are the kshatriyas, O son of Pritha, who are called to fight in such a battle that comes unsought as an open gate to heaven.

33) But if you refuse to engage in this righteous warfare, then forfeiting your own dharma and honor, you shall incur sin.

34) The world also will ever hold you in reprobation. To the honored, disrepute is surely worse than death.

35) The great chariot-warriors will believe that you have withdrawn from the battle through fear. And you will be lightly esteemed by them who have thought much of you.

36) your enemies also, cavilling at your great prowess, will say of you things that are not to be uttered. What could be more intolerable than this?

37) Dying you gain heaven; conquering you enjoy the earth. Therefore, O son of Kunti, arise, resolved to fight

38) Having made pain and pleasure, gain and loss, conquest and defeat, the same, engage then in battle. So shall you incur no sin.

39) The wisdom of self-realization has been declared unto you. Hearken now to the wisdom of yoga, endued with which, O son of Pritha, you shall break through the bonds of karma.

40) In this, there is no waste of the unfinished attempt, nor is there production of contrary results. Even very little of this dharma protects from the great terror.

41) In this, O scion of Kuru, there is but a single one-pointed determination. The purposes of the undecided are innumerable and many-branching.

42-44) O Partha, no set determination is formed in the minds of those that are deeply attached to pleasure and power, and whose discrimination is stolen away by the flowery words of the unwise, who are full of desires and look upon heaven as their highest goal and who, taking pleasure in the panegyric words of the Vedas, declare that there is nothing else. Their flowery words are exuberant with various specific rites as the means to pleasure and power and are the causes of [new] births as the result of their works [performed with desire].

45) The Vedas deal with the three gunas. Be free, O Arjuna, from the triad of the gunas, free from the pairs of opposites, ever-balanced, free from [the thought of] getting and keeping, and established in the self.

46) To the Brahmin who has known the self, all the Vedas are of so much use as a reservoir is, when there is a flood everywhere.

47) Your right is to work only; but never to the fruits thereof. Be not the producer of the fruits of [your] actions; neither let your attachment be towards inaction.

48) Being steadfast in yoga, O Dhananjaya, perform actions, abandoning attachment, remaining unconcerned as regards success and failure. This evenness of mind [in regard to success and failure] is known as yoga.

49) Word [with desire] is verily far inferior to that performed with the mind undisturbed by thoughts of results. O Dhananjaya, seek refuge in this evenness of mind. Wretched are they who act for results.

50) Endued with this evenness of mind, one frees oneself in this life, alike from vice and virtue. Devote yourself, therefore, to this yoga. Yoga is the very dexterity of work.

51) The wise, possessed of this evenness of mind, abandoning the fruits of their actions, freed for ever from the fetters of birth, go to that state which is beyond all evil.

52) When your intellect crosses beyond the taint of illusion, then shall you attain to indifference, regarding things heard and things yet to be heard.

53) When your intellect, tossed about by the conflict of opinions, has become immovable and firmly established in the self, then you shall attain self-realization.

Arjuna said:
54) What, O Keshava, is the description of the man of steady wisdom, merged in samadhi? How [on the other hand] does the man of steady wisdom speak, how sit, how walk?

The Blessed Lord said:

55) When a man completely casts away, O Partha, all the desires of the mind, satisfied in the self alone by the self, then is he said to be one of steady wisdom.

56) He whose mind is not shaken by adversity, who does not hanker after happiness, who has become free from affection, fear, and wrath, is indeed the muni of steady wisdom.

57) He who is everywhere unattached, not pleased at receiving good, nor vexed at evil, his wisdom is fixed.

58) When also, like the tortoise withdrawing its limbs, he can completely withdraw the senses from their objects, then his wisdom becomes steady.

59) Objects fall away from the abstinent man, leaving the longing behind. But his longing also ceases, who see the Supreme.

60) The turbulent senses, O son of Kunti, do violently snatch away the mind of even a wise man, striving after perfection.

61) The steadfast, having controlled them all, sits focussed on Me as the Supreme. His wisdom is steady, whose senses are under control.

62) Thinking of objects, attachment to them is formed in a man. From attachment longing, and from longing anger grows.

63) From anger comes delusion, and from delusion loss of memory. From loss of memory comes the ruin of discrimination, and from the ruin of discrimination he perishes.

64) But the self-controlled man, moving among objects with senses under restraint, and free from attraction and aversion, attains to tranquillity.

65) In tranquillity, all sorrow is destroyed. For the intellect of him, who is tranquil-minded, is soon established in firmness.

66) No knowledge [of the self] has the unsteady. Nor has he meditation. To the unmeditative there is no peace. And how can one without peace have happiness?

67) For, the mind, which follows in the wake of the wandering senses, carries away his discrimination, as a wind [carries away from its course] a boat on the waters.

68) Therefore, O mighty-armed, his knowledge is steady, whose senses are completely restrained from their objects.

69) That which is night to all beings, in that the self-controlled man wakes. This in which all being wake, is night to the self-seeing muni.

70) As into the ocean–brimful, and still–flow the waters, even so the muni into whom enter all desires, he, and not the desirer of desires, attains to peace.

71) That man who lives devoid of longing, abandoning all desires, without the sense of "I" and "mine," he attains to peace.

72) This is to have one's being in Brahma, O son of Pritha. None, attaining to this, becomes deluded. Being established therein, even at the end of life, a man attains to oneness with Brahman.

The Way of Action

Arjuna said:

1) If, O Janardana, according to You, knowledge is superior to action, why then, O Keshava, do You engage me in this terrible action?

2) With these seemingly conflicting words You are, as it were, bewildering my understanding. Tell me that one thing for certain by which I can attain to the highest.

The Blessed Lord said:

3) In the beginning [of creation], O sinless one, the twofold path of devotion was given by Me to this world: the path of knowledge for the meditating, the path of work for the active.

4) By non-performance of work none reaches worklessness; by merely giving up action no one attains to perfection.

5) Verily none can ever rest for even an instant without performing action; for all are made to act, helplessly indeed, by the gunas, born of Prakriti.

6) He who, restraining the organs of action, sit revolving in the mind thought regarding objects of sense, he, of deluded understanding, is called a hypocrite.

7) But, O Arjuna, he who, controlling by the senses by the mind, unattached, directs his organs of action to the path of work, excels.

8) Do you perform obligatory action; for action is superior to inaction; and even the bare maintenance of your body would not be possible if you are inactive.

9) The world is bound by actions other than those performed for the sake of yajna; do you, therefore, O son of Kunti, perform action for yajna alone, devoid of attachment.

10) The Prajapati, having in the beginning created mankind together with yajna, said, "By this shall you multiply: this shall be the milk cow of your desire."

11) "Cherish the devas with this, and may those devas cherish you: thus cherishing one another, you shall gain the highest good.

12) "The devas, cherished by yajna, will give you desired-for-objects." So, he who enjoys objects given by the devas without offering [in return] to them, is verily a thief.

13) The good, eating the remnants of yajna, are freed from all sins: but those who cook food [only] for themselves, those sinful ones eat sin.

14) From food come forth beings: from rain food is produced: from yajna 10 arises rain; and yajna is born of karma.

15) Know karma to have risen from the Veda, and the Veda from the Imperishable. Therefore the all-pervading Veda is ever centered in yajna.

16) He who here follows not the wheel thus set revolving, living in sin, and satisfied in the senses, O son of Pritha-he lives in vain.

17) But the man who is devoted to the self, and is satisfied with the self, and content in the self alone, has no obligatory duty.

18) He has no object in this world [to gain] by doing [an action], nor [does he incur any loss] by non-performance of action-nor has he [need of] depending on any being for any object.

19) Therefore, do you always perform actions which are obligatory, without attachment; by performing action without attachment, one attains to the highest.

20) Verily by action alone, Janaka and others attained perfection; also, simply with the view for the guidance of men, you should perform action.

21) Whatsoever the superior person does, that is followed by others. What he demonstrates by action, that people follow.

22) I have, O son of Pritha, no duty, nothing that I have not gained; and nothing that I have to gain in the three worlds; yet, I continue in action.

23) If ever I did not continue in work without relaxation, O son of Pritha, men would, in every way, follow in My wake.

24) If I did not do work, these worlds would perish. I should be the cause of the admixture [of races], and I should ruin these beings.

25) As do the unwise, attached to work, act, so should the wise act, O descendant of Bharata, [but] without attachment, desirous of the guidance of the world.

26) One should not unsettle the understanding of the ignorant, attached to action; the wise one, [himself] steadily acting, should engage [the ignorant] in all work.

27) The gunas of Prakriti perform all action. With the understanding deluded by egoism, man thinks, "I am the doer."

28) But one, with true insight into the domains of guna and karma, knowing that gunas as senses merely rest on gunas as objects, does not become attached.

29) Men of perfect knowledge should not unsettle [the understanding of] people of dull wit and imperfect knowledge, who deluded by the gunas of Prakriti attach [themselves] to the functions of the gunas.

30) Renouncing all actions to Me, with mind centered on the self, getting rid of hope and selfishness, fight-free from [mental] fever.

31) Those men who constantly practice this teaching of Mine, full of shraddha and without cavilling, they too are freed from work.

32) But those who decrying this teaching of Mine do not practice [it], deluded 11 in all knowledge, and devoid of discrimination, know them to be ruined.

33) Even a wise man acts in accordance with his own nature; beings follow nature: what can restraint to?

34) Attachment and aversion of the senses for their respective objects are natural: let none come under their sway: they are his foes.

35) Better is one's own dharma, [though] imperfect, than the dharma of another well-performed. Better is death in one's own dharma: the dharma of another is fraught with fear.

Arjuna said:

36) But impelled by what does man commit sin, though against his wishes, O Varshneya, constrained as it were by force?

The Blessed Lord said:

37) it is desire–it is anger, born of the Rajo-guna: of great craving, and of great sin; know this as the foe here [in this world].

38) As fire is enveloped by smoke, as a mirror by dust, as an embryo by the secundine, so is it covered by that.

39) Knowledge is covered by this, the constant foe of the wise, O son of Kunti, the unappeasable fire of desire.

40) The senses, the mind, and the intellect are said to be its abode: through these, it deludes the embodied by veiling his wisdom.

41) Therefore, O Bull of the Bharata race, controlling the senses at the outset, kill it–the sinful,the destroyer of knowledge and realization.

42) The senses are said to be superior [to the body]; the mind is superior to the senses; the intellect is superior to the mind; and that which is superior to the intellect is he [the atman].

43) Thus, knowing Him who is superior to the intellect, and restraining the self by the self, destroy, O mighty-armed, that enemy, the unseizable foe, desire.

The Way of Renunciation of Action in Knowledge

The Blessed Lord said:

1) I told this imperishable yoga to Vivasvat; Vivasvat told it to Manu; [and] Manu told it to Ikshvaku:

2) Thus handed down in regular succession, the royal sages knew it. This yoga, by long lapse of time, declined in this world, O scorcher of foes.

3) I have this day told you that same ancient yoga, [for] you are My devotee, and My friend, and this secret is profound indeed.

Arjuna said:

4) Later was Your birth, and that if Vivasvat prior; how then should I understand that You told this in the beginning?

The Blessed Lord said:

5) Many are the births that have been passed by Me and you, O Arjuna. I know them all, while you know not, O scorcher of foes.

6) Though I am unborn, of changeless nature and Lord of beings, yet subjugating My Prakriti, I come into being by My own Maya.

7) Whenever, O descendant of Bharata, there is decline of dharma, and rise of Adharma, then I body Myself forth.

8) For the protection of the good, for the destruction of the wicked, and for the establishment of dharma, I come into being.

9) He who thus knows, in true light, My divine birth and action, leaving the body, is not born again: he attains to Me, O Arjuna.

10) Freed from attachment, fear, and anger, absorbed in Me, taking refuge in Me, purified by the fire of knowledge, many have attained My Being.

11) In whatever way men worship Me, in the same way do I fulfil their desires; [it is] My path, O son of Pritha, [that] men tread, in all ways.

12) Longing for success in action, in this world, [men] worship the gods. Because success, resulting from action, is quickly attained in the human world.

13) The fourfold caste was created by Me, by the differentiation of guna and karma. Though I am the author thereof, know Me to be the non-doer, and changeless.

14) Actions do not taint Me, nor have I any thirst for the result of action. He who knows Me thus is not fettered by action.

15) Knowing thus, the ancient seekers after freedom also performed action. Do you, therefore, perform action, as did the ancients in olden times.

16) Even sages are bewildered as to what is action and what is inaction. I shall, therefore, tell you what action is, by knowing which you will be freed from evil.

17) For verily, [the true nature] even of action [enjoined by the shastras] should be known, as also [that] of forbidden action, and of inaction: the nature of karma is impenetrable.

18) He who sees inaction in action, and action in inaction is intelligent among men, he is a yogi and a doer of all action.

19) Whose undertakings are all devoid of plan and desire for results, and whose actions are burnt by the fire of knowledge, him the sages call wise.

20) Forsaking the clinging to fruits of action, ever satisfied, depending on nothing, though engaged in action, he does not do anything.

21) Without hope, the body and mind controlled, and all possessions relinquished, he does not suffer any evil consequences, by doing mere bodily action.

22) Content with what comes to him without effort, unaffected by the pairs of opposites, free from envy, even-minded in success and failure, though acting, he is not bound.

23) Devoid of attachment, liberated, with mind centered in knowledge, performing work for yajna alone, his whole karma dissolves away.

24) The process is Brahman, the clarified butter is Brahman, offered by Brahman in the fire of Brahman; by seeing Brahman in action, he reaches Brahman alone.

25) Some yogis perform sacrifices to devas alone, while others offer the self as sacrifice by the self in the fire of Brahman alone.

26) Some again offer hearing and other senses as sacrifice in the fire of control, while others offer sound and other sense-objects as sacrifice in the fire of the senses.

27) Some again offer all the actions of senses and the functions of the vital energy, as sacrifice in the fire of control in self, kindled by knowledge.

28) Others again offer wealth, austerity, and yoga, as sacrifice, while others, of self-restraint and rigid vows, offer study of the scriptures and knowledge, as sacrifice.

29) Yet some offer as sacrifice, the outgoing into the incoming breath, and the incoming into the outgoing, stopping the courses of the incoming and outgoing breaths, constantly practicing the regulation of the vital energy; while others yet of regulated food, offer in the pranas the functions thereof.

30-31) All of these are knowers of yajna, having their sins consumed by yajna, and eating of the nectar-the remnant of yajna-they go to the Eternal Brahman. [Even] this world is not for the non-performer of yajna, how then another, O best of the Kurus?

32) Various yajnas, like the above, are strewn in the storehouse of the Veda. Know them all to be born of action; and thus knowing, you shall be free.

33) Knowledge-sacrifice, O scorcher of foes, is superior to sacrifice [performed] with [material] objects. All action in its entirety, O Partha, attains its consummation in knowledge.

34) Know that, by prostrating yourself, by questions, and by service; the wise, those who have realized the Truth, will instruct you in that knowledge.

35) Knowing which, you shall not, O Pandava, again get deluded like this, and by which you shall see the whole of creation in [your] self and in Me.

36) Even if you are the most sinful among all the sinful, yet by the raft of knowledge alone you shall go across all sin.

37) As blazing fire reduces wood into ashes, so, O Arjuna, does the fire of knowledge reduce all karma to ashes.

38) Verily there exists nothing in this world purifying like knowledge. In good time, having reached perfection in yoga, one realizes that oneself in one's own heart.

39) The man with shraddha, the devoted, the master of one's senses, attains [this] knowledge. Having attained knowledge one goes at once to the Supreme Peace.

40) The ignorant, the man without shraddha, the doubting self, goes to destruction. The doubting self has neither this world, nor the next, nor happiness.

41) With work renounced by yoga and doubts rent asunder by knowledge, O Dhananjaya, actions do not bind him who is poised in the self.

42) Therefore, cutting with the sword of knowledge, this doubt about the self, born of ignorance, residing in your heart, take refuge in yoga. Arise, O Bharata!

The Way of Renunciation

Arjuna said:

1) Renunciation of action, O Krishna, you commend, and again, its performance. Which is the better one of these? Do You tell me decisively.

The Blessed Lord said:

2) Both renunciation and performance of action lead to freedom: of these, performance of action is superior to the renunciation of action.

3) He should be known a constant sannyasi, who neither likes nor dislikes: for, free from the pairs of opposites, O mighty-armed, he is easily set free from bondage.

4) Children, not the wise, speak of knowledge and performance of action as distinct. He who truly lives in one, gains the fruits of both.

5) The plane which is reached by the jnanis is also reached by the karma yogis. He who sees knowledge and performance of action as one alone sees.

6) Renunciation of action, O mighty-armed, is hard to attain to without performance of action; the man of meditation, purified by devotion to action, quickly goes to Brahman.

7) With the mind purified by devotion to performance of action, and the body conquered, and senses subdues, one who realizes one's self as the self in all beings, though acting, is not tainted.

8-9) The knower of Truth, [being] centered [in the self] should think, "I do nothing at all"–though seeing, hearing, touching, smelling, eating, going, sleeping, breathing, speaking, letting go, holding, opening, and closing the eyes–convinced that it is the senses that move among sense objects.

10) He who does actions forsaking attachment, resigning them to Brahman, is not soiled by evil, like unto a lotus leaf by water.

11) Devotees in the path of work perform action, only with body, mind, senses, and intellect, forsaking attachment, for the purification of the heart.

12) The well-poised, forsaking the fruit of action, attains peace, born of steadfastness; the unbalanced one, led by desire, is bound by being attached to the fruit (of action).

13) The subduer (of the senses), having renounced all actions by discrimination, rests happily in the city of the nine gates, neither acting, nor causing (others) to act.

14) Neither agency, nor actions does the Lord create for the world, nor (does he bring about) the union with the fruit of action. It is universal ignorance that does (it all).

15) The Omnipresent takes note of the merit or demerit of none. Knowledge is enveloped in ignorance, hence do beings get deluded.

16) But whose ignorance is destroyed by the knowledge of self–that knowledge of theirs, like the sun, reveals the Supreme (Brahman).

17) Those who have their intellect absorbed in That, whose self is That, whose steadfastness is in That, whose consummation is That, their impurities cleansed by knowledge, they attain to non-return (Moksha).

18) The knowers of the self look with an equal eye on a Brahmana endowed with learning and humility, a cow, an elephant, a dog, and a pariah.

19) (Relative) existence has been conquered by them, even in this world, whose mind rests in evenness, since Brahman is even and is without imperfection: therefore they indeed rest in Brahman.

20) Resting in Brahman, with intellect steady, and without delusion, the knower of Brahman neither rejoiceth on receiving what is pleasant, nor grieveth on receiving what is unpleasant.

21) With the heart unattached to external objects, he realizes the joy that is in the self. With the heart devoted to the meditation of Brahman, he attains undecaying happiness.

22) Since enjoyments that are contact-born are parents of misery alone, and with beginning and end, O son of Kunti, a wise man does not seek pleasure in them.

23) He who can withstand in this world, before the liberation from the body, the impulse arising from lust and anger, he is steadfast (in yoga), he is a happy man.

24) Whose happiness is within, whose relaxation is within, whose light is within, that Yogi alone, becoming Brahman, gains absolute freedom.

25) With imperfections exhausted, doubts dispelled, senses controlled, engaged in the good of all beings, the Rishis obtain absolute freedom.

26) Released from lust and anger, the heart controlled, the self realized, absolute freedom is for such Sannyasins, both here and hereafter.

27-28) Shutting out external objects; steadying the eyes between the eyebrows; restricting the even currents of prana and apana inside the nostrils; the senses, mind, and intellect controlled; with Moksha as the supreme goal; freed from desire, fear, and anger: such a man of moderation is verily free for ever.

29) Knowing Me as the dispenser of yajnas and asceticisms, as the Great Lord of all worlds, as the friend of all beings, he attains Peace.

The Way of Meditation

The Blessed Lord said:

1) He who performs his bounden duty without leaning to the fruit of action–he is a renouncer of action as well as of steadfast mind: not he who is without fire, nor he who is without action.

2) Know that to be devotion to action, which is called renunciation, O Pandava, for none becomes a devotee to action without forsaking Sankalpa.

3) For the man of meditation wishing to attain purification of heart leading to concentration, work is said to be the way: For him, when he has attained such (concentration), inaction is said to be the way.

4) Verily, when there is no attachment, either to sense-objects, or to actions, having renounced all Sankalpas, then is one said to have attained concentration.

5) A man should uplift himself by his own self, so let him not weaken this self. For this self is the friend of oneself, and this self is the enemy of oneself.

6) The self (the active part of our nature) is the friend of the self, for him who has conquered himself by this self. But to the unconquered self, this self is inimical, (and behaves) like (an external) foe.

7) To the self-controlled and serene, the Supreme Self is the object of constant realization, in cold and heat, pleasure and pain, as well as in honour and dishonour.

8) Whose heart is filled with satisfaction by wisdom and realization, and is changeless, whose senses are conquered, and to whom a lump of earth, stone, and gold are the same: that Yogi is called steadfast.

9) He attains excellence who looks with equal regard upon well-wishers, friends, foes, neutrals, arbiters, the hateful, the relatives, and upon the righteous and the unrighteous alike.

10) The yogi should constantly practise concentration of the heart, retiring into solitude, alone, with the mind and body subdued, and free from hope and possession.

11) Having established in a cleanly spot his seat, firm, neither too high nor too low, made of a cloth, a skin, and Kusha-grass, arranged in consecution.

12) There, seated on that seat, making the mind one-pointed and subduing the action of the imaging faculty and the senses, let him practise yoga for the purification of the heart.

13) Let him firmly hold his body, head, and neck erect and still, (with the eye-balls fixed, as if) gazing at the tip of his nose, and not looking around.

14) With the heart serene and fearless, firm in the vow of a Brahmachari, with the mind controlled, and ever thinking of Me, let his sit (in yoga) having Me as his supreme goal.

15) Thus always keeping the mind steadfast, the Yogi of subdued mind attains the peace residing in Me–the peace which culminates in Nirvana (Moksha).

16) (Success in) yoga is not for him who eats too much or too little–nor, O Arjuna, for him who sleeps too much or too little.

17) To him who is temperate in eating and recreation, in his effort for work, and in sleep and wakefulness, yoga becomes the destroyer of misery.

18) When the completely controlled mind rests serenely in the self alone, free from longing after all desires, then is one called steadfast (in the self).

19) "As a lamp in a spot sheltered from the wind does not flicker"–even such has been the simile used for a Yogi of subdued mind, practising concentration in the self.

20-23) When the mind, absolutely restrained by the practice of concentration, attains quietude, and when seeing the self by the self, one is satisfied in his own self; when he feels that infinite bliss–which is perceived by the (purified) intellect and which transcends the senses, and established wherein he never departs from his real state; and having obtained which, regards no other acquisition superior to that, and where established, he is not moved even by heavy sorrow; let that be known as the state, called by the name of yoga–a state of severance from the contact of pain. This yoga should be practised with perseverance, undisturbed by depression of heart.

24) Abandoning without reserve all desires born of Sankalpa, and completely restraining, by the mind alone, the whole group of senses from their objects in all directions;

25) With the intellect set in patience, with the mind fastened on the self, let him attain quietude by degrees: let him not think of anything.

26) Through wahtever reason the restless, unsteady mind wanders away, let him, curbing it from that, bring it under the subjugation of the self alone.

27) Verily, the supreme bliss comes to that Yogi, of perfectly tranquil mind, with passions quieted, Brahman-become, and freed from taint.

28) The Yogi, freed from tain (of good and evil), constantly engaging the mind thus, with ease attains the infinite bliss of contact with Brahman.

29) With the heart concentrated by yoga, with the eye of evenness for all things, he beholds the self in all beings and all beings in the self.

30) He who sees Me in all things, and sees all things in Me, he never becomes separated from Me, nor do I become separated from him.

31) Hw who being established in unity, worships Me, who am dwelling in all beings, whatever his mode of life, that yogi abides in Me.

32) He who judges of pleasure or pain everywhere, by the same standard as he applies to himself, that Yogi, O Arjuna, is regarded as the highest.

Arjuna said:

33) This yoga which has been taught by You, O slayer of Madhu, as characterized by evenness, I do not see (the possibility of) its lasting endurance, owing to restlessness (of the mind.)

34) Verily, the mind, O Krishna, is restless, turbulent, strong, and unyielding; I regard it quite as hard to achieve its control, as that of the wind.

The Blessed Lord said:

35) Without doubt, O mighty-armed, the mind is restless, and difficult to control; but through practice and renunciation, O son of Kunti, it may be governed.

36) Yoga is hard to be attained by one of uncontrolled self: such is My conviction; but the self-controlled, striving by right means can obtain it.

Arjuna said:

37) Though possess of shraddha but unable to control himself, with the mind wandering away from yoga, what end does one, failing to gain perfection in yoga, meet, O Krishna?

38) Does he not, fallen from both, perish, without support, like a rent cloud, O mighty-armed, deluded in the path of Brahman?

39) This doubt of mine, O Krishna, you should completely dispel; for it is not possible for any but you to dispel this doubt.

The Blessed Lord said:

40) Verily, O son of Pritha, there is destruction for him, neither here nor hereafter for, the doer of good, O my son, never comes to grief.

41) Having attained to the worlds of the righteous, and dwelling there for everlasting years, one falled from yoga reincarnates in the home of the pure and the prosperous.

42) Or else he is born into a family of wise yogis only; verily, a birth such as that is very rare to obtain in this world.

43) There he is united with the intelligence acquired in his former body, and strives more than before, for perfection, O son of the Kurus.

44) By that previous practice alone, he is borne on in spite of himself. Even the enquirer after yoga rises superior to the performer of Vedic actions

45) The Yogi, striving assiduously, purified of taint, gradually gaining perfection through many births, then reaches the highest goal.

46) The Yogi is regarded as superior to those who practice asceticism, also to those who have obtained wisdom (through the shastras). He is also superior to the performers of action (enjoined in the Vedas). Therefore, be a Yogi, O Arjuna!

47) And of all Yogis, he who with the inner self merged in Me, with shraddha devotes himself to Me, is considered by Me the most steadfast.

The Way of Knowledge With Realization

The Blessed Lord said:

1) With the mind intent on me, O son of Pritha, taking refuge in Me, and practicing yoga, how you shall without doubt know Me fully, that do you hear.

2) I shall tell you in full, of knowledge, speculative and practical, knowing which, nothing more here remains to be know.

3) One, perchance, in thousands of men, strives for perfection; and one perchance, among the blessed ones, striving thus, knows Me in reality.

4) Bhumi (earth, Ap (water), Anala (fire), Vayu (air), Kha (ether), intellect, and egoism: thus is My Prakriti divided eightfold.

5) This is the lower (Prakriti). But different from it, know, O mighty-armed, My higher Prakriti–the principle of self-consciousness, by which this universe is sustained.

6) Know that these (two Prakritis) are the womb of all beings, I am the origin and dissolution of the whole universe.

7) Beyond Me, O Dhananjaya, there is naught. All this is strung in Me, as a row of jewels on a thread.

8) I am the sapidity in water, O son of Kunti; I, the radiance in the moon and the sun; I am the Om in all the Vedas, sound in Akasha, and manhood in men.

9) I am the sweet fragrance in earth, and the brilliance in fire am I; the life in all beings, and the austerity am I in ascetics.

10) Know me, O son of Pritha, as the eternal seed of all beings. I am the intellect of the intelligent, and the heroism of the heroic.

11) Of the strong, I am the strength devoid of desire and attachment. I am, O bull among the Bharatas, desire in beings, unopposed to dharma.

12) And whatever states pertaining to sattwa, and those pertaining to rajas, and to tamas, know them to proceed from Me alone; still I am not in them, but they are in Me.

13) Deluded by these states, the modifications of the three gunas (of Prakriti), all this world does not know Me who is beyond them, and immutable.

14) Verily, this divine illusion of Mine, constituted of the gunas, is difficult to cross over; those who devote themselves to Me alone, cross over this illusion.

15) They do not devote themselves to Me–the evil-doers, the deluded, the lowest of men, deprived of discrimination by Maya, and following the way of the Asuras.

16) Four kinds of virtuous men worship Me, O Arjuna-the distressed, the seeker of knowledge, the seeker of enjoyment, and the wise, O bull among the Bharatas.

17) Of them, the wise man, ever-steadfast, (and fired) with devotion to the One, excels; for supremely dear am I to the wise, and he is dear to Me.

18) Noble indeed are they all, but the wise man I regard as My very self; for with the mind steadfast, he is established in Me alone, as the supreme goal.

19) At the end of many births, the man of wisdom takes refuge in Me, realizing that all this is Vasudeva (the innermost self). Very rare is that great soul.

20) Others, again, deprived of discrimination by this or that desire, following this or that rite, devote themselves to other gods, led by their own natures.

21) Whatsoever form any devotee seeks to worship with shraddha-the shraddha of his do I make unwavering.

22) Endued with that shraddha, he engages in the worship of that, and from it, gains his desires-these being verily dispensed by Me alone.

23) But the fruit (accruing) to these men of little understanding is limited. The worshippers of the devas go to the devas; My devotees too come to me.

24) The foolish regard Me, the unmanifested, as come into manifestation, not knowing My supreme state-immutable and transcendental.

25) Veiled by the illusion born of the congress of the gunas, I am not manifest to all. This deluded world knows Me not-the Unborn, the Immutable.

26) I know, O Arjuna, the beings of the whole past, and the present, and the future, but Me none knoweth.

27) By the delusion of the pairs of opposites, arising from desire and aversion, O descendant of Bharata, all beings fall into delusion at birth, O scorcher of foes.

28) Those men of virtuous deeds, whose sin has come to an end-they, freed from the delusion of the pairs of opposites, worship Me with firm resolve.

29) Those who strive for freedom from old age and death, taking refuge in Me-they know Brahman, the whole of Adhyatma, and karma in its entirety.

30) Those who know Me with the Adhibhuta, the Adhidaiva, and the Adhiyajna, (continue to) know Me even at the time of death, steadfast in mind.

The Way to the Imperishable Brahman

Arjuna said:

1) What is the Brahman, what is Adhyatma, what is karma, O best of Purushas? What is called Adhibhuta, and what Adhidaiva?

2) Who, and in what way, is Adhiyajna here in this body, O destroyer of Madhu? And how are You known at the time of death, by the self-controlled?

The Blessed Lord said:

3) The Imperishable is the Supreme Brahman. Its dwelling in each individual body is called Adhyatma; the offering in sacrifice which causes the genesis and support of beings, is called karma.

4) The perishable adjunct is the Adhibhuta, and the Indweller is the Adhidaivata; I alone am the Adhiyajna here in this body, O best of the embodied.

5) And he who at the time of death, meditating on Me alone, goes forth, leaving the body, attains My Being: there is no doubt about this.

6) Remembering whatever object, at the end, he leaves the body, that alone is reached by him, O son of Kunti, (because) of his constant thought of that object.

7) Therefore, at all times, constantly remember Me, and fight. With mind and intellect absorbed in Me, you shall doubtless come to Me.

8) With the mind not moving towards anything else, made steadfast by the method of habitual meditation, and dwelling on the Supreme, Resplendent Purusha, O son of Pritha, one goes to Him. 9-

10) The Omniscient, the Ancient, the Overruler, minuter than an atom, the Sustainer of all, of form inconceivable, self-luminous like the sun, and beyond the darkness of Maya–he who meditates on Him thus, at the time of death, full of devotion, with the mind unmoving, and also by the power of yoga, fixing the whole prana betwixt the eyebrows, he goes to that Supreme, Resplendent Purusha.

11) What the knowers of the Veda speak of as Imperishable, what the selfcontrolled (Sannyasis), freed from attachment enter, and to gain which goal they live the life of a Brahmachari, that I shall declare unto thee in brief.

12-13) Controlling all the senses, confining the mind in the heart, drawing the prana into the head, occupied in the practice of concentration, uttering the one-syllabled "Om"–the Brahman, and meditating on Me–he who so departs, leaving the body, attains the Supreme Goal.

14) I am easily attainable by that ever-steadfast Yogi who remembers Me constantly and daily, with a single mind, O son of Pritha.

15) Reaching the highest perfection and having attained Me, the great-souled ones are no more subject to rebirth–which is the home of pain, and ephemeral.

16) All the worlds, O Arjuna, including the realm of Brahma, are subject to return, but after attaining Me, O son of Kunti, there is no rebirth.

17) They who know (the true measure of) day and night, know the day of Brahma, which ends in a thousand Yugas, and the night which (also) ends in a thousand Yugas.

18) At the approach of (Brahma's) day, all manifestations proceed from the unmanifested state; at the approach of night, they merge verily into that alone, which is called the unmanifested.

19) The very same multitude of beings (that existed in the preceding day of Brahma), being born again and again, merge, in spite of themselves, O son of Pritha, (into the unmanifested), at the approach of night, and re-manifest at the approach of day.

20) But beyond this unmanifested, there is that other Unmanifested, Eternal Existence–That which is not destroyed at the destruction of all beings.

21) What has been called Unmanifested and Imperishable, has been described as the Goal Supreme. That is My highest state, having attained which, there is no return.

22) And that Supreme Purusha is attainable, O son of Pritha, by whole-souled devotion to Him alone, in Whom all beings dwell, and by Whom all this is pervaded.

23) Now I shall tell thee, O bull of the Bharatas, of the time (path) travelling in which, the Yogis return, (and again of that, taking which) they do not return.

24) Fire flame, daytime, the bright fortnight, the six months of the Northern passage of the sun–taking this path, the knowers of Brahman go to Brahman.

25) Smoke, night-time, the dark fortnight, the six months of the Southern passage of the sun–taking this path the Yogi, attaining the lunar light, returns.

26) Truly are these bright and dark paths of the world considered eternal: one leads to non-return; by the other, one returns.

27) No Yogi, O son of Pritha, is deluded after knowing these paths. Therefore, O Arjuna, be steadfast in yoga, at all times.

28) Whatever meritorious effect is declared (in the Scriptures) to accrue from (the study of) the Vedas, (the performance of) yajnas, (the practice of) austerities and gifts–above all this rises the Yogi, having known this, and attains to the primeval, supreme Abode.

The Way of the Kingly Knowledge and the Kingly Secret

The Blessed Lord said:

1) To thee, who dost not carp, verily shall I now declare this, the most profound knowledge, united with realization, having known which, you shall be free from evil (Samsara).

2) Of sciences, the highest; of profundities, the deepest; of purifiers, the supreme, is this; realizable by direct perception, endowed with (immense) merit, very easy to perform, and of an imperishable nature.

3) Persons without shraddha for this dharma, return, O scorcher of foes, without attaining Me, to the path of rebirth fraught with death.

4) All this world is pervaded by Me in My unmanifested form: all beings exist in Me, but I do not dwell in them.

5) Nor do beings exists in Me, (in reality), behold My divine yoga! Bringing forth and supporting the beings, My Self does not dwell in them.

6) As the mighty wind, moving always everywhere, rests ever in the Akasha, know that even so do all beings rest in Me.

7) At the end of a Kalpa, O son of Kunti, all beings go back to My Prakriti: at the beginning of (another) Kalpa, I send them forth again.

8) Animating My Prakriti, I project again and again this whole multitude of beings, helpless under the sway of Prakriti.

9) These acts do not bind Me, sitting as one neutral, unattached to them, O Dhananjaya.

10) By reason of My proximity, Prakriti produces all this, the moving and the unmoving; the world wheels round and round, O son of Kunti, because of this.

11) Unaware of My higher state, as the great Lord of being, fools disregard Me, dwelling in the human form.

12) Of vain hopes, of vain works, of vain knowledge, and senseless, they verily are possessed of the delusive nature of Rakshasas and Asuras.

13) But the great-souled ones, O son of Pritha, possessed of the Divine Prakriti, knowing Me to be the origin of beings and immutable, worship Me with a single mind.

14) Glorifying Me always and striving with firm resolve, bowing down to Me in devotion, always steadfast, they worship Me.

15) Others, too, sacrificing by the yajna of knowledge (I.e., seeing the self in all), worship Me the All-Formed, as one, as distinct, as manifold.

16) I am the Kratu, I the Yajna, I the Svadha, I the Aushadha, I the Mantra, I the Ajya, I the fire, and I the oblation.

17) I am the Father of this world–the Mother, the Sustainer, the Grandfather, the Purifier, the (one) thing to be known, (the syllable) Om, and also the Rik, Saman, and Yajus.

18) The Goal, the Supporter, the Lord, the Witness, the Abode, the Refuge, the Friend, the Origin, the Dissolution, the Substratum, the Storehouse, the Seed immutable.

19) (As the sun) I give heat; I withhold and send forth rain; I am immortality and also death; being and non-being am I, O Arjuna!

20) The knowers of the three Vedas, worshipping Me by yajna, drinking the Soma, and (thus) being purified from sin, pray for passage to heaven; reaching the holy world of the Lord of the devas, they enjoy in heaven the divine pleasures of the devas.

21) Having enjoyed the vast Svarga-world, they enter the mortal world, on the exhaustion of their merit: Thus, abiding by the injunctions of the three (Vedas), desiring desires, they (constantly) come and go.

22) Persons who, meditating on Me as non-separate, worship Me in all beings, to them thus ever zealously engaged, I carry what they lack and preserve what they already have.

23) Even those devotees, who endued with shraddha, worship other gods, they too worship Me alone, O son of Kunti, (but) by the wrong method

24) For I alone am the Enjoyer, and Lord of all yajnas; but because they do not know Me in reality, they return, (to the mortal world).

25) Votaries of the devas go to the devas' to the Pitris, go their votaries; to the Bhutas, go the Bhuta worshippers; My votaries too come unto Me.

26) Whoever with devotion offers Me a leaf, a flower, a fruit, or water, that I accept–the devout gift of the pure-minded.

27) Whatever you do, whatever you eat, whatever you off in sacrifice, whatever you give away, whatever austerity ou practice, O son of Kunti, do that as an offering unto Me.

28) Thus shall you be freed from the bondages of actions, bearing good and evil results: with the heart steadfast in the yoga of renunciation, and liberated you shall come unto Me.

29) I am the same to all beings: to Me there is none hateful or dear. But those who worship Me with devotion, are in Me, and I too am in them.

30) If even a very wicked person worships Me, with devotion to none else, he should be regarded as good, for he has rightly resolved.

31) Soon does he become righteous, and attain eternal Peace, O son of Kunti; boldly can you proclaim, that My devotee is never destroyed.

32) For, taking refuge in Me, they also, O son of Pritha, who might be of inferior birth-women, Vaishyas, as well as Shudras-even they attain to the Supreme Goal.

33) What need to mention holy Brahmanas, and devoted Rajarshis! Having obtained this transient, joyless world, worship Me.

34) Fill your mind with Me, be My devotee, sacrifice unto Me, bow down to Me; thus having made your heart steadfast in Me, taking Me as the Supreme Goal, you shall come to Me.

Glimpses of the Divine Glory

The Blessed Lord said:

1) Again, O mighty-armed, listen to My supreme word, which I wishing your welfare, will tell thee who art delighted (to hear Me).

2) Neither the hosts of devas, nor the great Rishis, know My origin, for in every way I am the source of all the devas and the great Rishis.

3) He who knows Me, birthless and beginningless, the great Lord of worlds–he, among mortals, is undeluded, he is freed from all sins.

4-5) Intellect, knowledge, non-delusion, forbearance, truth, restraint of the external senses, calmness of heart, happiness, misery, birth, death, fear, as well as fearlessness, non-injury, evenness, contentment, austerity, benevolence, good name, (as well as) ill-fame–(these) different kinds of qualities of beings arise from Me alone.

6) The seven great Rishis as well as the four ancient manus, possessed of powers like Me (due to their thoughts being fixed on Me), were born of (My) mind; from them are these creatures in the world.

7) He who in reality knows these manifold manifestations of My being and (this) yoga power of Mine, becomes established in the unshakable yoga; there is no doubt about it.

8) I am the origin of all, from Me everything evolves–thus thinking, the wise worship Me with loving consciousness.

9) With their minds wholly in Me, with their senses absorbed in Me, enlightening one another, and always speaking of Me, they are satisfied and delighted.

10) To them, ever steadfast and serving Me with affection, I give that buddhiyoga by which they come unto Me.

11) Out of mere compassion for them, I, abiding in their hearts, destroy the darkness (in them) born of ignorance, by the luminous lamp of knowledge.

Arjuna said:

12-13) The Supreme Brahman, the Supreme Abode, the Supreme Purifier, are You. All the Rishis, the deva-Rishi Narada as well as Asita, Devala, and Vyasa have declared You as the Eternal, the self-luminous Purusha, the first Deva, Birthless, and All-pervading. So also you yourself say to me.

14) I regard all this that you say to me as true, O Keshava. Verily, O Bhagavan, neither the devas nor the Danavas know Your manifestation.

15) Verily, you yourself know yourself by yourself, O Supreme Purusha, O Source of being, O Lord of beings, O Deva of Devas, O Ruler of the World.

16) You should indeed speak, without reserve of Your divine attributes by which, filling all these worlds, you existest.

17) How shall I, O Yogi, meditate ever to know You? In what things, O Bhagavan, are you to be thought of by me?

18) Speak to me again in detail, O Janardana, of your yoga-powers and attributes; for I am never satiated in hearing the ambrosia (of Your speech).

The Blessed Lord said:

19) I shall speak to thee now, O best of the Kurus, of my divine attributes, according to their prominence; there is no end to the particulars of My manifestation.

20) I am the Self, O Gudakesha, existent in the heart of all beings; I am the beginning, the middle, and also the end of all beings.

21) Of the Adityas, I am Vishnu; of luminaries, the radiant Sun; of the winds, I am Marichi; of the asterisms, the Moon.

22) I am the Sama-Veda of the Vedas, and Vasava (Indra) of the gods; of the senses I am the mind and intelligence in living beings am I.

23) And of the Rudras I am Shankara; of the Yakshas and Rakshasas, the Lord of wealth (Kubera); of the Vasus I am Pavaka; and of mountains, Meru am I.

24) And of priests, O son of Pritha, know Me the chief, Brihaspati; of generals, I am Skanda; of bodies of water, I am the ocean.

25) Of the great Rishis I am Bhrigu; of words I am the one syllable "Om;" of yajnas I am the yajna of japa (silent repetition); of immovable things the Himalaya.

26) Of all trees (I am) the Ashvattha, and Narada of deva-Rishis; Chitraratha of Gandharvas am I, and the Muni Kapila of the perfected ones.

27) Know me among horses as Uchchaishsravas, Amrita-born; of lordly elephants Airavata, and of men the king.

28) Of weapons I am the thunderbolt, of cows I am Kamadhuk; I am the Kandarpa, the cause of offspring; of serpents I am Vasuki.

29) And Ananta of snakes I am, I am Varuna of water-beings; and Aryaman of Pitris I am, I am Yama of controllers.

30) And Prahlada am I of Diti's progeny, of measurers I am Time; and of beasts I am the lord of beasts [lion], and Garuda of birds.

31) Of purifiers I am the wind, Rama of warriors am I; of fishes I am the shark, of streams I am Jahnavi (the Ganga).

32) Of manifestations I am the beginning, the middle and also the end; of all knowledges I am the knowledge of the self, and Vada of disputants.

33) Of letters the letter A am I, and Dvandva of all compounds; I alone am the inexhaustible Time, I the Sustainer (by dispensing fruits of actions) All-formed.

34) An I am the all-seizing Death, and the prosperity of those who are to be prosperous; of the feminine qualities (I am) Fame, Prosperity (or beauty, Inspiration, Memory, Intelligence, Constancy and Forbearance.

35) Of Samas also I am the Brihat-Sama, of metres Gayatri am I; of months I am Margashirsha, of seasons the flowery season.

36) I am the gambling of the fraudulent, I am the power of the powerful; I am victory, I am effort, I am sattwa of the sattwic.

37) Of the Vrishnis I am Vasudeva; of the Pandavas, Dhananjaya; and also of the Munis I am Vyasa; of the sages, Ushanas the sage.

38) Of punishers I am the sceptre; of those who seek to conquer, I am statesmanship; and also of things secret I am silence, and the knowledge of knowers am I.

39) And whatsoever is the seed of all beings, that also am I, O Arjuna. There is no being, whether moving or unmoving, that can exist without Me.

40) There is no end of My divine attributes, O scorcher of foes; but this is a brief statement by Me of the particulars of My divine attributes.

41) Whatever being there is great, prosperous, or powerful, that know to be a product of a part of My splendour.

42) Or what avails thee to know all this diversity, O Arjuna? (Know this that) I exist, supporting this whole world by a portion of Myself.

The Vision of the Universal Form

Arjuna said:

1) By the supremely profound words, on the discrimination of self, that have been spoken by You out of compassion towards me, this my delusion is gone.

2) Of You, O lotus-eyed, I have heard at length, of the origin and dissolution of beings, as also Your inexhaustible greatness.

3) So it is, O Supreme Lord,! as You have declared Yourself. (Still) I desire to see Your Ishvara-Form, O Supreme Purusha.

4) If, O Lord, You think me capable of seeing it, the, O Lord of Yogis, show me Your immutable Self.

The Blessed Lord said:

5) Behold, O son of Pritha, by hundreds and thousands, My different forms celestial, of various colours and shapes.

6) Behold the Adityas, the Vasus, the Rudras, the twin Ashvins, and the Maruts; behold, O descendant of Bharata, many wonders never seen before.

7) See now, O Gudakesha, in this My body, the whole universe centred in one–including the moving and the unmoving–and all else that you desirest to see.

8) But you cannot see me with these eyes of yours; I give thee supersensuous sight; behold My supreme yoga power. **Sanjaya said:**

9) Having thus spoken, O King, Hari, the Great Lord of Yoga, showed unto the son of Pritha, His Supreme Ishvara-Form:

10) With numerous mouths and eyes, with numerous wondrous sights, with numerous celestial ornaments, with numerous celestial weapons uplifted;

11) Wearing celestial garlands and apparel, anointed with celestial-scented unguents, the All-wonderful Resplendent, Boundless, and All-formed.

12) If the splendour of a thousand suns were to rise up simultaneously in the sky, that would be like the splendour of that Mighty Being.

13) There in the body of the God of gods, the son of Pandu then saw the whole universe resting in one, with its manifold divisions.

14) Then Dhananjaya, filled with wonder, with his hairs standing on end, bending down his head to the Deva in adoration, spoke with joined palms.

Arjuna said:

15) I see all the devas, O Deva, in Your body, and hosts of all grades of beings; Brahma, the Lord, seated on the lotus, and all the Rishis and celestial serpents.

16) I see You of boundless form on every side with manifold arms, stomachs, mouths, and eyes; neither the end nor the middle, nor also the beginning of You do I see, O Lord of the universe, O Universal Form.

17) I see You with diadem, club, and discus; a mass of radiance shining everywhere, very hard to look at, all around blazing like burning fire and sun, and immeasurable.

18) You are the Imperishable, the Supreme Being, the one thing to be known. You are the great Refuge of this universe; You are the undying Guardian of the Eternal dharma, You are the Ancient Purusha, I ween.

19) I see You without beginning, middle, or end, infinite in power, of manifold arms; the sun and the moon Your eyes, the burning fire Your mouth; heating the whole universe with Your radiance.

20) This space betwixt heaven and earth and all the quarters are filled by You alone; having seen this, Your marvelous and awful form, the three worlds are trembling with fear, O Great-souled One.

21) Verily, into You enter these hosts of devas; some extol You in fear with joined palms; "May it be well!" thus saying, bands of great Rishis and Siddhas praise You with splendid hymns.

22) The Rudras, Adityas, Vasus, Sadhyas, Vishva-devas, the two Ashvins, Maruts, Ushmapas, and hosts of Gandharvas, Yakshas, Asuras, and Siddhas–all these are looking at You, all quite astounded.

23) Having seen Your immeasurable Form–with many mouths and eyes, O mighty-armed, with many arms, thighs, and feet, with many stomachs, and fearful with many tusks–the worlds are terrified, and so am I.

24) On seeing You touching the sky, shining in many a colour, with mouths wide open, with large fiery eyes, I am terrified at heart, and find no courage nor peace, O Vishnu.

25) Having seen Your mouths, fearful with tusks, (blazing) like Pralaya-fires, I know not the four quarters, nor do I find peace; have mercy, O Lord of the devas, O Abode of the universe.

26-27) All those sons of Dhritarashtra, with hosts of monarchs, Bhishma, Drona, and Sutaputra, with the warrior chiefs of ours, enter precipitately into Your mouth, terrible with tusks and fearful to behold. Some are found sticking in the interstices of Your teeth, with their heads crushed to powder.

28) Verily, as the many torrents of rivers flow towards the ocean, so do those heroes in the world of men enter Your fiercely flaming mouths.

29) As moths precipitately rush into a blazing fire only to perish, even so do these creatures also precipitately rush into Your mouths only to perish.

30) Swallowing all the worlds on every side with Your flaming mouths, You are licking Your lips. Your fierce rays, filling the whole world with radiance, are burning, O Vishnu!

31) Tell me who You are, fierce in form. Salutation to You, O Supreme Deva! have mercy. I desire to know You, O Primeval One. I know not indeed Your purpose.

The Blessed Lord said:

32) I am the mighty world-destroying Time, here made manifest for the purpose of infolding the world. Even without thee, none of the warriors arrayed in the hostile armies shall live.

33) Therefore arise and acquire fame. Conquer the enemies, and enjoy the unrivalled dominion. Verily by Myself have they been already slain; be merely an apparent cause, O Savyasachin (Arjuna).

34) Drona, Bhishma, Jayadratha, Karna as well as other brave warriors–these already killed by Me, do you kill. Be not distressed with fear; fight, and you shall conquer your enemies in battle. **Sanjaya said:**

35) Having heard this speech of Keshava, the diademed one (Arjuna), with joined palms, trembling, prostrated himself, and again addresssed Krishna in a choked voice, bowing down, overwhelmed with fear.

Arjuna said:

36) It is meet, O Hrishikesha, that the world is delighted and rejoices in Your praise, that rakshasas fly in fear to all quarters and all the hosts of Siddhas bow down to You in adoration.

37) And why should they not, O Great-souled One, bow to You, greater than, and the Primal Cause of even Brahma, O Infinite Being, O Lord of the devas, O Abode of the universe? You are the Imperishable, the Being and the non-Being, (as well as) That which is Beyond (them).

38) You are the Primal Deva, the Ancient Purusha; You are the Supreme Refuge of this universe, You are the Knower, and the One Thing to be known; You are the Supreme goal. By You is the universe pervaded, O boundless Form.

39) You are Vayu, Yama, Agni, Varuna, the Moon, Prajapati, and the Greatgrandfather. Salutation, salutation to You, a thousand times, and again and again salutation, salutation to You!

40) Salutation to You before and behind, salutation to You on every side, O All! You, infinite in power and infinite in prowess, pervadest all; wherefore You are All.

41-42) Whatever I have presumptuously said from carelessness or love, addressing You as "O Krishna, O Yadava, O friend," regarding You merely as a friend, unconscious of this Your greatness–in whatever way I may have been disrespectful to You in fun, while walking, reposing, sitting, or at meals, when alone (with You), O Achyuta, or in company–I implore You, Immeasurable One, to forgive all this.

43) You are the Father of the world, moving and unmoving; the object of its worship; greater than the great. None there exists who is equal to You in the three worlds; who then can excel You, O You of power incomparable?

44) So prostrating my body in adoration, I crave Your forgiveness, Lord adorable! As a father forgiveth his son, friend a dear friend, a eloed one his love, even so should You forgive me, O Deva.

45) Overjoyed am I to have seen what I saw never before; yet my mind is distracted with terror. Show me, O Deva, only that form of Yours. Have mercy, O Lord of Devas, O Abode of the universe.

46) Diademed, bearing a mace and a discus, You I desire to see as before. Assume that same four-armed Form, O You of thousand arms, of universal Form.

The Blessed Lord said:
47) Graciously have I shown to thee, O Arjuna, this Form supreme, by My own yoga power, this resplendent, primeval, infinite, universal Form of Mine, which hathnot been seen before by anyone else.

48) Neither by the study of the Veda and yajna, nor by gifts, nor by rituals, nor by severe austerities, am I in such Form seen, in the world of men, by any other than thee, O great hero of the Kurus.

49) Be not afraid nor bewildered, having beheld this Form of Mine, so terrific. With your fears dispelled and with gladdened heart, now see again this former Form of Mine. **Sanjaya said:**

50) So Vasudeva, having thus spoken to Arjuna, showed again His own Form; and the Great-souled One, assuming His gently Form, pacified him who was terrified.

Arjuna said:

51) Having seen this Your gentle human Form, O Janardana, my thoughts are now composed, and I am restored to my nature.

The Blessed Lord said:

52) Very hard indeed it is to see this Form of Mine which you have hast seen. Even the devas ever long to behold this Form.

53) Neither by the Vedas, nor by austerity, nor by gifts, nor by sacrifice can I be seen as you have seen Me.

54) But by single-minded devotion I may in this form, be known, O Arjuna, and seen in reality, and also entered into O scorcher of foes.

55) He who does work for Me alone and has Me for his goal, is devoted to Me, is freed from attachment, and bears enmity towards no creature-he entereth into Me, O Pandava.

The Way of Devotion

Arjuna said:

1) Those devotees who, ever-steadfast, thus worship You, and those also who worship the Imperishable, the Unmanifested–which of them are better versed in yoga?

The Blessed Lord said:

2) Those who, fixing their mind on Me, worship Me, ever-steadfast, and endowed with supreme shraddha, they in My opinion are the best versed in yoga.

3-4) But those also, who worship the Imperishable, the Indefinable, the Unmanifested, the Omnipresent, the Unthinkable, the Unchangeable, the Immovable, the Eternal–having subdued all the senses, even-minded everywhere, engaged in the welfare of all beings–verily they read only Myself.

5) Greater is their trouble whose minds are set on the Unmanifested; for the goal of the Unmanifested is very hard for the embodied to reach.

6-7) But those who worship Me, resigning all actions in Me, regarding me as the Supreme Goal, meditating on Me with single-minded yoga–to those whose mind is set on Me, verily, I become ere long, O son of Pritha, the Saviour out of the ocean of the mortal Samsara.

8) Fix your mind on Me only, place your intellect in Me: (then) you shall no doubt live in Me hereafter.

9) If you are unable to fix your mind steadily on Me, then by abhyasa-yoga do you seek to reach Me, O Dhananjaya.

10) If also you are unable to practice Abhyasa, be intent on doing actions for my sake. Even by doing actions for My sake, you shall attain perfection.

11) If you are unable to do even this, then taking refuge in Me, abandon the fruit of all action, being self-controlled.

12) Better indeed is knowledge than (blind) Abhyasa; meditation (with knowledge) is more esteemed than (mere) knowledge; than meditation the renunciation of the fruit of action; peace immediately follows renunciation.

13-14) He who hates no creature, and is friendly and compassionate towards all, who is free from the feelings of "I" and "mine," even-minded in pain and pleasure, forbearing, ever content, steady in meditation, self-controlled, and possessed of firm conviction, with mind and intellect fixed on Me–he who is thus devoted to Me, is dear to Me.

15) He by whom the world is not agitated and who cannot be agitated by the world, who is freed from joy, envy, fear, and anxiety–he is dear to Me.

16) He who is free from dependence, who is pure, prompt, unconcerned, untroubled, renouncing every undertaking–he who is thus devoted to Me, is dear to Me.

17) He who neither rejoices, nor hates, nor grieves, nor desires, renouncing good and evil, full of devotion, he is dear to Me.

18-19) He who is the same to friend and foe, and also in honor and dishonor; who is the same in heat and cold, and in pleasure and pain; who is free from attachment; to whom censure and praise are equal; who is silent, contend with anything, homeless, steady-minded, full of devotion–that man is dear to Me.

20) And they who follow this Immortal Dharma, as described above, endued with shraddha, regarding Me as the Supreme Goal, and devoted–they are exceedingly dear to Me.

The Discrimination of the Kshetra and the Kshetrajna

Arjuna said: Prakriti and Purusha, also the kshetra and the knower of the kshetra, knowledge, and that which ought to be known-these, O Keshava, I desire to learn.

The Blessed Lord said:

1) This body, O son of Kunti, is called kshetra, and he who knows it is called kshetrajna by those who know of them (kshetra and kshetrajna).

2) Me do you also know, O descendant of Bharata, to be kshetrajna in all kshetras. The knowledge of kshetra and kshetrajna is considered by Me to be the knowledge.

3) What the kshetra is, what is properties are, what its modifications are, what effects arise from what causes, and also who He is and what His powers are, that hear from Me in brief.

4) (This truth) has been sung by Rishis in many ways, in various distinctive chants, in passages indicative of Brahman, full of reasoning, and convincing.

5-6) The great Elements, Egoism, Intellect, as also the Unmanifested (Mula Prakriti), the ten senses and the one (mind), and the five objects of the senses; desire, hatred, pleasure, pain, the aggregate, intelligence, fortitude-the kshetra has been thus briefly described with its modifications.

7) Humility, unpretentiousness, non-injury, forbearance, uprightness, service to the teacher, purity, steadiness, self-control;

8) The renunciation of sense-objects, and also absence of egoism; reflection on the evils of birth, death, old age, sickness, and pain;

9) Non-attachment, non-identification of self with son, wife, home, and the rest, and constant even-mindedness in the occurrence of the desirable and the undesirable;

10) Unswerving devotion to Me by the yoga of non-separation, resort to sequestered places, distaste for the society of men;

11) Constant application to spiritual knowledge, understanding of the end of true knowledge; this is declared to be knowledge, and what is opposed to it is ignorance.

12) I shall describe that which has to be known, knowing which one attains to immortality, the beginningless Supreme Brahman. It is called neither being nor non-being.

13) With hands and feet everywhere, with eyes, heads, and mouths everywhere, with ears everywhere in the universe–That exists pervading all.

14) Shining by the functions of all the senses, yet without the senses; Absolute, yet sustaining all; devoid of gunas, yet their experiencer.

15) Without and within (all) beings; the unmoving and also the moving; because of Its subtlety incomprehensible; It is far and near.

16) Impartible, yet It exists as if divided in beings: It is to be known as sustaining beings; and devouring, as well as generating (them).

17) The Light even of lights, It is said to be beyond darkness; Knowledge, and the One Thing to be known, the Goal of knowledge, dwelling in the hearts of all.

18) Thus kshetra, knowledge, and that which has to be known, have been briefly stated. Knowing this, My devotee is fitted for My state.

19) Know that Prakriti and Purusha are both beginningless; and know also that all modifications and gunas are born of Prakriti.

20) In the production of the body and the senses, Prakriti is said to be the cause; in the experience of pleasure and pain, Purusha is said to be the cause.

21) Purusha seated in Prakriti, experiences the gunas born of Prakriti; the reason of his birth in good and evil wombs is his attachment to the gunas.

22) And the Supreme Purusha in this body is also called the Looker-on, the Permitter, the Supporter, the Experiencer, the Great Lord, and the Highest Self.

23) He who thus knows the Purusha and Prakriti together with the gunas, whatever his life, is not born again.

24) Some by meditation behold the self in their own intelligence by the purified heart, others by the path of knowledge, others again by karma-yoga.

25) Others again not knowing thus, worship as they have heard from others. Even these go beyond death, regarding what they have heard as the Supreme Refuge.

26) Whatever being is born, the moving or the unmoving, O bull of the Bharatas, know it to be from the union of kshetra and kshetrajna.

27) He sees, who sees the Supreme Lord, existing equally in all beings, deathless in the dying.

28) Since seeing the Lord equally existent everywhere, he injures not self by self, and so goes to the highest Goal.

29) He sees, who sees that all actions are done by Prakriti alone and that the self is actionless.

30) When he sees the separate existence of all being inherent in the One, and their expansion from That (One) alone, he then becomes Brahman.

31) Being without beginning and devoid of gunas, this Supreme Self, immutable, O son of Kunti, though existing in the body neither acts nor is affected.

32) As the all-pervading Akasha, because of its subtlety, is not tainted, so the self existent everywhere in the body is not tainted.

33) As the one sun illumines all this world, so does He who abides in the kshetra, O descendant of Bharata, illumine the whole kshetra.

34) They who thus with the eye of knowledge perceive the distinction between the kshetra and the kshetrajna, and also the emancipation from the Prakriti of beings, they go to the Supreme.

The Discrimination of the Three Gunas

The Blessed Lord said:

1) Again I shall tell you that supreme knowledge which is above all knowledge, having known which all the Munis have attained to high perfection after this life.

2) They who, having devoted themselves to this knowledge, have attained to My Being, are neither born at the time of creation, nor are they troubled at the time of dissolution.

3) My womb is the great Prakriti; in that I place the germ; from thence, O descendant of Bharata, is the birth of all beings.

4) Whatever forms are produced, O son of Kunti, in all the wombs, the great Prakriti is their womb, and I the seed-giving Father.

5) Sattwa, rajas, and tamas-these gunas, O mighty-armed, born of Prakriti, bind fast in the body the indestructible embodied one.

6) Of these sattwa, because of its stainlessness, luminous and free from evil, binds, O sinless one, by attachment to happiness, and by attachment to knowledge.

7) Know rajas to be of the nature of passion, giving rise to thirst and attachment; it binds fast, O son of Kunti, the embodied one, by attachment to action.

8) And know tamas to be born of ignorance, stupefying all embodied beings; it binds fast, O descendant of Bharata, by miscomprehension, indolence, and sleep.

9) Sattwa attaches to happiness, and rajas to action, O descendant of Bharata; while tamas, verily, shrouding discrimination, attaches to miscomprehension.

10) Sattwa arises, O descendant of Bharata, predominating over rajas and tamas; likewise rajas over sattwa and tamas; so, tamas over sattwa and rajas.

11) When through every sense in this body, the light of intelligence shines, then it should be known that sattwa is predominant.

12) Greed, activity, the undertaking of actions, unrest, longing-these arise when rajas is predominant, O bull of the Bharatas.

13) Darkness, inertness, miscomprehension, and delusion-these arise when tamas is predominant, O descendant of Kuru.

14) If the embodied one meets death when sattwa is predominant, then he attains to the spotless regions of the worshippers of the Highest.

15) Meeting death in rajas he is born among those attached to action; so dying in tamas, he is born in the wombs of the irrational.

16) The fruit of good action, they say, is Sattvika and pure; verily, the fruit of rajas is pain, and ignorance is the fruit of tamas.

17) From sattwa arises wisdom, and from rajas greed; miscomprehension, delusion and ignorance arise from tamas.

18) The sattwa-abiding go upwards; the rajasic dwell in the middle; and the tamasic, abiding in the function of the lowest guna, go downwards.

19) When the seer beholds no agent other than the gunas and knows That which is higher than the gunas, he attains to My being.

20) The embodied one having gone beyond these three gunas, out of which the body is evilved, is freed from birth, death, decay, and pain, and attains to immortality.

Arjuna said:
21) By what marks, O Lord, is he (known) who has gone beyond these three gunas? What is his conduct, and how does he pass beyond these three gunas?

The Blessed Lord said:
22) He who hates not the appearance of light (the effect of sattwa), activity (the effect of rajas), and delusion (the effect of tamas), (in his own mind), O Pandava, nor longs for them when absent;

23) He who, sitting like one unconcerned, is moved not by the gunas, who knowing that the gunas operate, is self-centered and swerves not;

24) Alike in pleasure and apin, self-abiding, regarding a clod of earth, a stone and gold alike; the same to agreeable and disagreeable, firm, the same in censure and praise;

25) The same in honor and disgrace, the same to friend and foe, relinquishing all undertakings–he is said to have gone beyond the gunas.

26) And he who serves Me with unswerving devotion, he, going beyond the gunas, is fitted for becoming Brahman.

27) For I am the abode of Brahman, the Immortal and Immutable, of everlasting dharma and of Absolute Bliss.

The Way to the Supreme Spirit

The Blessed Lord said:

1) They speak of an eternal Ashvattha rooted above and branching below whose leaves are the Vedas; he who knows it, is a Veda-knower.

2) Below and above spread its branches, nourished by the gunas; sense-objects are its buds; and below in the world of man stretch forth the roots, originating action.

3-4) Its form is not here perceived as such, neither its end, nor its origin, nor its existence. Having cut asunder this firm-rooted Ashvattha with the strong axe of non-attachment–then that Goal is to be sought for, going whither they (the wise) do not return again. I seek refuge in that Primeval Purusha whence streamed forth the Eternal Activity.

5) Free from pride and delusion, with the evil of attachment conquered, ever dwelling in the self, with desires completely receded, liberated from the pairs of opposites known as pleasure and pain, the undeluded reach that Goal Eternal.

6) That the sun illumines not, nor the moon, nor fire; that is My Supreme Abode, going whither they return not.

7) An eternal portion of Myself having become a living soul in the world of life, draws (to itself) the (five) senses with mind for the sixth, abiding in Prakriti.

8) When the Lord obtains a body and when He leaves it, He takes these and goes, as the wind takes the scents from their seats (the flowers).

9) Presiding over the ear, the eye, the touch, the taste, and the smell, as also the mind, He experiences objects.

10) While transmigrating (from one body to another), or residing (in the same) or experiencing, or when united with the gunas–the deluded do not see Him; but those who have the eye of wisdom behold Him.

11) The Yogis striving (for perfection) behold Him dwelling in themselves; but the unrefined and unintelligent, even though striving, see Him not.

12) The light which residing in the sun illumines the whole world, that which is in the moon and in the fire–know that light to be Mine.

13) Entering the earth with My energy, I support all beings, and I nourish all the herbs, becoming the watery moon.

14) Abiding in the body of living beings as (the fire) Vaishvanara, I, associated with prana and apana, digest the fourfold food.

15) I am centered in the hearts of all; memory and perception as well as their loss come from Me. I am verily that which has to be known by all the Vedas, I indeed am the Author of the Vedanta, and the Knower of the Veda am I.

16) There are two Purushas in the world–the Perishable and the Imperishable. All beings are the Perishable, and the Kutastha is called Imperishable.

17) But (there is) another, the Supreme Purusha, called the Highest Self, the immutable Lord, who pervading the three worlds, sustains them.

18) As I transcend the Perishable and am above even the Imperishable, therefore am I in the world and in the Veda celebrated as Purushottama (the Highest Purusha).

19) He who, free from delusion, thus knows Me, the Highest Spirit, he knowing all, worships Me with all his heart, O descendant of Bharata.

20) Thus, O sinless one, has this most profound teaching been imparted by Me. Knowing this one attains the highest intelligence and will have accomplished all one's duties, O descendant of Bharata.

The Classification of the Divine and the Nondivine Attributes

The Blessed Lord said:

1) Fearlessness, purity of heart, steadfastness in knowledge and yoga; almsgiving, control of the senses, yajna, reading of the shastras, austerity, uprightness;

2) Non-injury, truth, absence of anger, renunciation, tranquillity, absence of calumny, compassion to beings, uncovetousness, gentleness, modesty, absence of fickleness;

3) Boldness, forgiveness, fortitude, purity, absence of hatred, absence of pride; these belong to one born for a divine state, O descendant of Bharata.

4) Ostentation, arrogance, and self-conceit, anger as also harshness and ignorance, belong to one who is born, O Partha, for an asuric state.

5) The divine state is deemed to make for liberation, the asuric for bondage; grieve not, O Pandava, you are born for a divine state.

6) There are two types of beings in this world, the divine and the asuric. The divine have been described at length; hear from Me, O Partha, of the asuric.

7) The persons of asuric nature know not what to do and what to refrain from; neither is purity found in them nor good conduct, nor truth.

8) They say, "The universe is without truth, without a (moral) basis, without a God, brought about by mutual union, with lust for its cause; what else?"

9) Holding this view, these ruined souls of small intellect and fierce deeds, rise as the enemies of the world for its destruction.

10) Filled with insatiable desires, full of hypocrisy, pride, and arrogance, holding evil ideas through delusion, they work with impure resolve.

11) Beset with immense cares ending only with death, regarding gratification of lust as the highest, and feeling sure that that is all;

12) Bound by a hundred ties of hope, given over to lust and wrath, they strive to secure by unjust means hoards of wealth for sensual enjoyment.

13) "This today has been gained by me; this desire I shall obtain; this is mind, and this wealth also shall be mine in the future.

14) "That enemy has been slain by me, and others also shall I slay. I am the Lord, I enjoy, I am successful, powerful, and happy.

15) "I am rich and well-born. Who else is equal to me? I will sacrifice, I will give, I will rejoice." Thus deluded by ignorance,

16) Bewildered by many a fancy, covered by the meshes of delusion, addicted to the gratification of lust, they fall down into a foul hell.

17) Self-conceited, haughty, filled with the pride and intoxication of wealth, they perform sacrifices in name, out of ostentation, disregarding ordinance.

18) Possessed of egoism, power, insolence, lust, and wrath, these malignant people hate Me (the self within) in their own bodies and those of others.

19) These malicious and cruel evil-doers, most degraded of men, I hurl perpetually into the wombs of Asuras only, in these worlds.

20) Obtaining the asuric wombs, and deluded birth after birth, not attaining to Me, they thus fall, O son of Kunti, into a still lower condition.

21) Triple is this gate of hell, destructive of the self–lust, anger and greed; therefore one should forsake these three.

22) The man who has got beyond these three gates of darkness, O son of Kunti, practices what is good for himself, and thus goes to the Goal Supreme.

23) He who, setting aside the ordinance of the shastra, acts under the impulse of desire, attains not to perfection, nor happiness, nor the Goal Supreme.

24) So let the shastra be your authority in ascertaining what ought to be done and what ought not to be done. Having known what is said in the ordinance of the shastra, ou should act here.

The Enquiry into the Threefold Shraddha

Arjuna said:

1) Those who, setting aside the ordinance of the shastra, perform sacrifice with shraddha, what is their condition, O Krishna? (Is it) sattwa, rajas, or tamas?

The Blessed Lord said:

2) Threefold is the shraddha of the embodied, which is inherent in their nature–the satwic, rajasic, and the tamasic. Do you hear of it.

3) The shraddha of each is according to his natural disposition, O descendant of Bharata. The man consists of his shraddha; he verily is what his shraddha is.

4) Sattwic men worship the devas; rajasika, the yakshas and the rakshasa; the others–the tamasic men–the pretas and the hosts of bhutas.

5-6) Those men who practice severe austerities not enjoined by the shastras, given to ostentation and egoism, endowed with the power of lust and attachment, torture senseless as they are, all the organs in the body, and Me dwelling in the body within; know them to be of asuric resolve.

7) The food also which is liked by each of them is threefold, as also yajna, austerity, and almsgiving. Do you hear this, their distinction.

8) The foods which augment vitality, energy, strength, health, cheerfulness, and appetite, which are savory and oleaginous, substantial and agreeable, ae liked by the sattwic.

9) The foods that are bitter, sour, saline, excessively hot, pungent, dry, and burning, are liked by the rajasic, and are productive of pain, grief, and disease.

10) That which is stale, tasteless, stinking, cooked overnight, refuse, and impure, is the food liked by the tamasic.

11) That yajna is sattwic which is performed by men desiring no fruit, as enjoined by ordinance, with their mind fixed on the yajna only, for its own sake.

12) That which is performed, O best of the Bharatas, seeking for fruit and for ostentation, know it to be a rajasic yajna.

13) The yajna performed without heed to ordinance, in which no food is distributed, which is devoid of mantras, gifts, and shraddha, is said to be tamasic.

14) Worship of the devas, the twice-born, the gurus, and the wise; purity, straightforwardness, continence, and non-injury are called the austerity of the body.

15) Speech which causes no vexation, and is true, as also agreeable and beneficial, and regular study of the Vedas–these are said to form the austerity of speech.

16) Serenity of mind, kindliness, silence, self-control, honesty of motive–this is called the mental austerity.

17) This threefold austerity practiced by steadfast men, with great Shraddha, desiring no fruit, is said to be sattwic.

18) That austerity which is practiced with the object of gaining welcome, honor, and worship, and with ostentation, is here said to be rajasic, unstable, and transitory.

19) That austerity which is practiced out of a foolish notion, with self-torture, or for the purpose of ruining another, is declared to be tamasic.

20) "To give is right"–gift given with this idea, to one who does no service in return, in a fit place and to a worthy person, that gift is held to be sattwic.

21) And what is given with a view to receiving in return, or looking for the fruit, or again reluctantly, that gift is held to be rajasic.

22) The gift that is given at the wrong place or time, to unworthy persons, without regard or with disdain, that is declared to be tamasic.

23) "Om, Tat, Sat": this has been declared to be the triple designation of Brahman. By that were made of old the Brahmanas, the Vedas, and the yajnas.

24) Therefore, uttering "Om" are the acts of sacrifice, gift, and austerity as enjoined in the ordinances, always begun by the followers of the Vedas.

25) Uttering "Tat," without aiming at fruits, are the various acts of yajna, austerity, and gift performed by the seekers of Moksha.

26) The word "Sat" is used in the sense of reality and of goodness; and so also, O Partha, the word "Sat" is used in the sense of an auspicious act.

27) Steadiness in yajna, austerity, and gift is also called "Sat": as also action in connection with these (or, action for the sake of the Lord) is called "Sat."

28) Whatever is sacrificed, given, or performed and whatever austerity is practiced without shraddha, it is called Asat, O Partha; it is naught here or hereafter.

The Way of Liberation in Renunciation

Arjuna said:

1) I desire to know severally, O mighty-armed, the truth of sannyasa, O Hrishikesha, as also of tyaga, O slayer of Keshi.

The Blessed Lord said:

2) The renunciation of kamya actions the sages understand as sannyasa: the wise declare the abandonment of the fruit of all works as tyaga.

3) Some philosophers declare that all actions should be relinquished as an evil, whilst others (say) that the work of yajna, gift, and austerity should not be relinquished.

4) Hear from Me the final truth about relinquishment, O best of the Bharatas. For relinquishment has been declared to be of three kinds, O tiger among men.

5) The work of yajna, gift, and austerity should not be relinquished, but it should indeed be performed; (for) yajna, gift, and austerity are purifying to the wise.

6) But even these works, O Partha, should be performed, leaving attachment and the fruits; such is My best and certain conviction.

7) But the renunciation of obligatory action is not proper. Abandonment of the same from delusion is declared to be tamasic.

8) He who from fear of bodily trouble relinquishes action, because it is painful, thus performing a rajasic relinquishment, he obtains not the fruit thereof.

9) When obligatory work is performed, O Arjuna, only because it ought to be done, leaving attachment and fruit, such relinquishment is regarded as sattwic.

10) The relinquisher endued with sattwa and a steady understanding and with his doubts dispelled, hates not a disagreeable work nor is attached to an agreeable one.

11) Actions cannot be entirely relinquished by an embodied being, but he who relinquishes the fruits of actions is called a relinquisher.

12) The threefold fruit of action–disagreeable, agreeable, and mixed–accrues to non-relinquishers after death, but never to relinquishers.

13) Learn from Me, O mighty-armed, these five causes for the accomplishment of all works as declared in the wisdom which is the end of all action;

14) The body, the agent, the various senses, the different functions of a manifold kind, and the presiding divinity, the fifth or these;

15) Whatever action a man performs by his body, speech, and mind–whether right or the reverse–these five are its causes.

16) Such being the case, he who through a non-purified understanding looks upon his self, the Absolute, as the agent–he of perverted mind sees not.

17) He who is free from the notion of egoism, whose intelligence is not affected (by good or evil), though he kills these people, he kills not, nor is bound (by the action).

18) Knowledge, the known and the knower form the threefold cause of action. The instrument, the object, and the agent are the threefold basis of action.

19) Knowledge, action and agent are declared in the Sankhya philosophy to be of three kinds only, from the distinction of gunas: hear them also duly.

20) That by which the one indestructible Substance is seen in all being, inseparate in the separated, know that knowledge to be sattwic.

21) But that knowledge which sees in all beings various entities of distinct kinds as different from one another, know that knowledge as rajasic

22) Whilst that which is confined to one single effect as if it were the whole, without reason, without foundation in truth, and trivial–that is declared to be tamasic.

23) An ordained action done without love or hatred by one not desirous of the fruit and free from attachment, is declared to be sattwic.

24) But the action which is performed desiring desires, or with self-conceit and with much effort, is declared to be rajasic.

25) That action is declared to be tamasic which is undertaken through delusion, without heed to the consequence, loss (of power and wealth), injury (to others), and (one's own) ability.

26) An agent who is free from attachment, non-egotistic, endued with fortitude and enthusiasm, and unaffected in success or failure, is called sattwic.

27) He who is passionate, desirous of the fruits of action, greedy, malignant, impure, easily elated or dejected, such an agent is called rajasic.

28) Unsteady, vulgar, arrogant, dishonest, malicious, indolent, desponding, and procrastinating, such an agent is called tamasic.

29) Hear the triple distinction of intellect and fortitude, according to the gunas, as I declare them exhaustively and severally, O Dhananjaya.

30) That which knows the paths of work and renunciation, right and wrong action, fear and fearlessness, bondage and liberation, that intellect, O Partha, is sattwic.

31) That which has a distorted apprehension of dharma and its opposite and also of right action and its opposite, that intellect, O Partha, is rajasic.

32) That which, enveloped in darkness, regards adharma as dharma and views all things in a perverted light, that intellect, O Partha, is tamasic.

33) The fortitude by which the functions of the mind, the prana, and the senses, O Partha, are regulated, that fortitude, unswerving through yoga, is sattwic.

34) But the fortitude by which one regulates (one's mind) to dharma, desire, and wealth, desirous of the fruit of each from attachment, that fortitude, O Partha, is rajasic.

35) That by which a stupid man does not give up sleep, fear, grief, despondency, and also overweening conceit, that fortitude, O Partha, is tamasic.

36) And now hear from Me, O bull of the Bharatas, of the threefold happiness that one learns to enjoy by habit, and by which one comes to the end of pain.

37) That which is like poison at first, but like nectar at the end; that happiness is declared to be sattwic, born of the translucence of intellect due to self-realization.

38) That which arises from the contact of object with sense, at first like nectar, but at the end like poison, that happiness is declared to be rajasic.

39) That happiness which begins and results in self-delusion arising from sleep, indolence, and miscomprehension, that is declared to be tamasic.

40) There is no entity on earth, or again in heaven among the devas, that is devoid of these three gunas, born of Prakriti.

41) Of Brahmanas and kshatriyas and vaishyas, as also of shudras, O scorcher of foes, the duties are distributed according to the Gunas born of their own nature.

42) The control of the mind and the senses, austerity, purity, forbearance, and also uprightness, knowledge, realization, belief in a hereafter–these are the duties of the brahmanas, born of (their own) nature.

43) Prowess, boldness, fortitude, dexterity, and also not flying from battle, generosity and sovereignty are the duties of the kshatriyas, born of (their own) nature.

44) Agriculture, cattle-rearing, and trade are the duties of the Vaishyas, born of (their own) nature; and action consisting of service is the duty of the shudras, born of (their own) nature.

45) Devoted each to his own duty, man attains the highest perfection. How engaged in his own duty, he attains perfection, that hear.

46) From whom is the evolution of all beings, by whom all this is pervaded, worshipping Him with his own duty, a man attains perfection.

47) Better is one's own dharma, (though) imperfect than the dharma of another well-performed. He who does the duty ordained by his own nature incurs no evil.

48) One should not relinquish, O son of Kunti, the duty to which one is born, though it is attended with evil; for, all undertakings are enveloped by evil, as fire by smoke.

49) He who intellect is unattached everywhere, who has subdued his heart, whose desires have fled, he attains by renunciation to the supreme perfection, consisting of freedom from action.

50) Learn from Me in brief, O son of Kunti, how reaching such perfection, he attains to Brahman, that supreme consummation of knowledge.

51) Endued with a pure intellect; subduing the body and the senses with fortitude; relinquishing sound and such other sense-objects; abandoning attraction and hatred;

52) Resorting to a sequestered spot; eating but little; body, speech, and mind controlled; ever engaged in meditation and concentration; possessed of dispassion;

53) Forsaking egoism, power, pride, lust, wrath, and property; freed from the notion of "mine;" and tranquil-he is fit for becoming Brahman.

54) Brahman-become, tranquil-minded, he neither grieves nor desires; the same to all beings, he attains to supreme devotion unto Me.

55) By devotion he knows me in reality, what and who I am; then having known Me in reality, he forthwith enters into Me.

56) Even doing all actions always, taking refuge in Me-by My grace he attains to the eternal, immutable State.

57) Resigning mentally all deeds to Me, having Me as the highest goal, resorting to buddhi-yoga do you ever fix your mind on Me.

58) Fixing your mind on Me, you shall, by My grace, overcome all obstacles; but if from self-conceit you will not hear Me, you shall perish.

59) If, filled with self-conceit, you think, "I will not fight," vain is this your resolve; your prakriti will constrain you.

60) Fettered, O son of Kunti, by your own karma, born of your own nature, what you, from delusion, desire not to do, you shall have to do in spite of yourself.

61) The Lord, O Arjuna, dwells in the hearts of all beings, causing all beings, by His Maya, to revolve, (as if) mounted on a machine.

62) Take refuge in Him with all your heart, O Bharata; by His grace you shall attain supreme peace (and) the eternal abode.

63) Thus has wisdom, more profound than all profundities, been declared to you by Me; reflecting over it fully, act as you like.

64) Hear again My supreme word, the profoundest of all; because you are dearly beloved of Me, therefore, will I speak what is good to you.

65) Occupy your mind with Me, be devoted to Me, sacrifice to Me, bow down to Me. You shall reach Myself; truly do I promise unto you, (for) you are dear to Me.

66) Relinquishing all dharmas take refuge in Me alone; I will liberate you from all sins; grieve not.

67) This is never to be spoken by you to one who is devoid of austerities or devotion, nor to one who does not render service, nor to one who cavils at Me.

68) He who with supreme devotion to Me will teach this deeply profound philosophy to My devotees, shall doubtless come to Me alone.

69) Nor among men is there any who does dearer service to Me, nor shall there be another on earth dearer to Me, than he.

70) And he who will study this sacred dialogue of ours, by him shall I have been worshipped by the yajna of knowledge; such is My conviction.

71) And even that man who hears this, full of shraddha and free from malice, he too, liberated shall attain to the happy worlds of those of righteous deeds.

72) Has this been heard by you, O Partha, with an attentive mind? Has the delusion of your ignorance been destroyed, O Dhananjaya?

Arjuna said:
73) Destroyed is my delusion, and I have gained my memory through Your grace, O Achyuta. I am firm; my doubts are gone. I will do Your word.

Sanjaya said:
74) Thus have I heard this wonderful dialogue between Vasudeva and the high-souled Partha, causing my hair to stand on end.

75) Through the grace of Vyasa have I heard this supreme and most profound Yoga, direct from Krishna, the Lord of Yoga, Himself declaring it.

76) O King, as I remember and remember this wonderful and holy dialogue between Keshava and Arjuna, I rejoice again and again.

77) And as I remember and remember that most wonderful form of Hari, great is my wonder, O King; and I rejoice again and again. 78) Wherever is Krishna, the Lord of Yoga, wherever is Partha, the wielder of the bow, there are prosperity, victory, expansion, and sound policy: such is my conviction.

The Greatness of the Gita

Arjuna said:

1) I desire to know severally, O mighty-armed, the truth of Sannyâsa, O Hrishikesha, as also of Tyâga, O slayer of Keshi.

The Blessed Lord said:

2) The renunciation of Kâmya actions, the sages understand as. Sannyâsa: the wise declare the abandonment of the fruits of all works as Tyâga.

3) Some philosophers declare that all action should be relinquished as an evil, whilst others (say) that the work of Yajna, gift and austerity should not be relinquished.

4) Hear from Me the final truth about relinquishment, O best of the Bhâratas. For relinquishment has been declared to be of three kinds, O tiger among men.

5) The work of Yajna, gift and austerity should not be relinquished, but it should indeed be performed; (for) Yajna, gift and austerity are purifying to the wise.

6) But even these works, O Pârtha, should be performed, leaving attachment and the fruits;—such is My best and certain conviction.

7) But the renunciation of obligatory action is not proper. Abandonment of the same from delusion is declared to be Tâmasika.

8) He who from fear of bodily trouble relinquishes action, because it is painful, thus performing a Râjasika relinquishment, he obtains not the fruit thereof.

9) When obligatory work is performed, O Arjuna, only because it ought to be done, leaving attachment and fruit, such relinquishment is regarded as Sâttvika.

10) The relinquisher endued with Sattva and a steady understanding and with his doubts dispelled, hates not a disagreeable work nor is attached to an agreeable one.

11) Actions cannot be entirely relinquished by an embodied being, but he who relinquishes the fruits of action is called a relinquisher.

12) The threefold fruit of action—disagreeable, agreeable and mixed,—accrues to non-relinquishers after death, but never to relinquishers.

13) Learn from Me, O mighty-armed, these five causes for the accomplishment of all works as declared in the wisdom which is the end of all action:

14) The body, the agent, the various senses, the different functions of a manifold kind, and the presiding divinity, the fifth of these;

15) Whatever action a man performs by his body, speech and mind—whether right or the reverse—these five are its causes.

16) Such being the case, he who through a non-purified understanding looks upon his Self, the Absolute, as the agent, he of perverted mind sees not.

17) He who is free from the notion of egoism, whose intelligence is not affected (by good or evil), though he kills these people, he kills not, nor is bound (by the action);

18) Knowledge, the known and the knower form the threefold cause of action. The instrument, the object and the agent are the threefold basis of action.

19) Knowledge, action and agent are declared in the Sânkhya philosophy to be of three kinds only, from the distinction of Gunas: hear them also duly.

20) That by which the one indestructible Substance is seen in all beings, inseparate in the separated, know that knowledge to be Sâttvika.

21) But that knowledge which sees in all beings various entities of distinct kinds as different from one another, know thou that knowledge as Râjasika.

22) Whilst that which is confined to one single effect as if it were the whole, without reason, without foundation in truth, and trivial,—that is declared to be Tâmasika.

23) An ordained action done without love or hatred by one not desirous of the fruit and free from attachment, is declared to be Sâttvika.

24) But the action which is performed desiring desires, or with self-conceit and with much effort, is declared to be Râjasika.

25) That action is declared to be Tâmasika which is undertaken through delusion, without heed to the consequence, loss (of power and wealth), injury (to others) and (one's own) ability.

26) An agent who is free from attachment, non-egotistic, endued with fortitude and enthusiasm and unaffected in success or failure, is called Sâttvika.

27) He who is passionate, desirous of the fruits of action, greedy, malignant, impure, easily elated or dejected, such an agent is called Râjasika.

28) Unsteady, vulgar, arrogant, dishonest, malicious, indolent, desponding and procrastinating, such an agent is called Tâmasika.

29) Hear thou the triple distinction of intellect and fortitude, according to the Gunas, as I declare them exhaustively and severally, O Dhananjaya.

30) That which knows the paths of work and renunciation, right and wrong action, fear and fearlessness, bondage and liberation, that intellect, O Pârtha, is Sâttvika.

31) That which has a distorted apprehension of Dharma and its opposite and also of right action and its opposite, that intellect, O Pârtha, is Râjasika.

32) That which enveloped in darkness regards Adharma as Dharma and views all things in a perverted light, that intellect, O Pârtha, is Tâmasika.

33) The fortitude by which the functions of the mind, the Prâna and the senses, O Pârtha, are regulated, that fortitude, unswerving through Yoga, is Sâttvika.

34) But the fortitude by which one regulates (one's mind) to Dharma, desire and wealth, desirous of the fruit of each from attachment, that fortitude, O Pârtha, is Râjasika.

35) That by which a stupid man does not give up sleep, fear, grief, despondency and also overweening conceit, that fortitude, O Pârtha, is Tâmasika.

36) And now hear from Me, O bull of the Bhâratas, of the threefold happiness. That happiness which one learns to enjoy by habit, and by which one comes to the end of pain;

37) That which is like poison at first, but like nectar at the end; that happiness is declared to be Sâttvika, born of the translucence of intellect due to Self-realisation.

38) That which arises from the contact of object with sense, at first like nectar, but at the end like poison, that happiness is declared to be Râjasika.

39) That happiness which begins and results in self-delusion arising from sleep, indolence and miscomprehension, that is declared to be Tâmasika.

40) There is no entity on earth, or again in heaven among the Devas, that is devoid of these three Gunas, born of Prakriti.

41) Of Brâhmanas and Kshatriyas and Vaishyas, as also of Sudras, O scorcher of foes, the duties are distributed according to the Gunas born of their own nature.

42) The control of the mind and the senses, austerity, purity, forbearance, and also uprightness, knowledge, realisation, belief in a hereafter,—these are the duties of the Brâhmanas, born of (their own) nature.

43) Prowess, boldness, fortitude, dexterity, and also not flying from battle, generosity and sovereignty are the duties of the Kshatriyas, born of (their own) nature.

44) Agriculture, cattle-rearing and trade are the duties of the Vaishyas, born of (their own) nature; and action consisting of service is the duty of the Sudras, born of (their own) nature.

45) Devoted each to his own duty, man attains the highest perfection. How engaged in his own duty, he attains perfection, that hear.

46) From whom is the evolution of all beings, by whom all this is pervaded, worshipping Him with his own duty, a man attains perfection.

47) Better is one's own Dharma, (though) imperfect, than the Dharma of another well-performed. He who does the duty ordained by his own nature incurs no evil.

48) One should not relinquish, O son of Kunti, the duty to which one is born, though it is attended with evil; for, all undertakings are enveloped by evil, as fire by smoke.

49) He whose intellect is unattached everywhere, who has subdued his heart, whose desires have fled, he attains by renunciation to the supreme perfection, consisting of freedom from action.

50) Learn from Me in brief, O son of Kunti, how reaching such perfection, he attains to Brahman, that supreme consummation of knowledge.

51) Endued with a pure intellect, subduing the body and the senses with fortitude, relinquishing sound and such other sense-objects, abandoning attraction and hatred;

52) Resorting to a sequestered spot, eating but little, body, speech and mind controlled, ever engaged in meditation and concentration, possessed of dispassion;

53) Forsaking egoism, power, pride, lust, wrath and property, freed from the notion of "mine," and tranquil, he is fit for becoming Brahman.

54) Brahman-become, tranquil-minded, he neither grieves nor desires; the same to all beings, he attains to supreme devotion unto Me.

55) By devotion he knows Me in reality, what and who I am; then having known Me in reality, he forthwith enters into Me.

56) Even doing all actions always, taking refuge in Me,—by My grace he attains to the eternal, immutable State.

57) Resigning mentally all deeds to Me, having Me as the highest goal, resorting to Buddhi-Yoga do thou ever fix thy mind on Me.

58) Fixing thy mind on Me, thou shalt, by My grace, overcome all obstacles; but if from self-conceit thou wilt not hear Me, thou shalt perish.

59) If filled with self-conceit thou thinkest, "I will not fight," vain is this thy resolve; thy Prakriti will constrain thee.

60) Fettered, O son of Kunti, by thy own Karma, born of thy own nature, what thou, from delusion, desirest not to do, thou shalt have to do in spite of thyself.

61) The Lord, O Arjuna, dwells in the hearts of all beings, causing all beings, by His Mâyâ, to revolve, (as if) mounted on a machine.

62) Take refuge in Him with all thy heart, O Bhârata; by His grace shalt thou attain supreme peace (and) the eternal abode.

63) Thus has wisdom more profound than all profundities, been declared to. thee by Me; reflecting over it fully, act as thou likest.

64) Hear thou again My supreme word, the profoundest of all; because thou art dearly beloved of Me, therefore will I speak what is good to thee.

65) Occupy thy mind with Me, be devoted to Me, sacrifice to Me, bow down to Me. Thou shalt reach Myself; truly do I promise unto thee, (for) thou art dear to Me.

66) Relinquishing all Dharmas take refuge in Me alone; I will liberate thee from all sins; grieve not. 66

67) This is never to be spoken by thee to one who is devoid of austerities or devotion, nor to one who does not render service, nor to one who cavils at Me.

68) He who with supreme devotion to Me will teach this deeply profound philosophy to My devotees, shall doubtless come to Me alone.

69) Nor among men is there any who does dearer service to Me, nor shall there be another on earth dearer to Me, than he.

70) And he who will study this sacred dialogue of ours, by him shall I have been worshipped by the Yajna of knowledge; such is My conviction.

71) And even that man who hears this, full of Shraddhâ and free from malice, he too, liberated, shall attain to the happy worlds of those of righteous deeds.

72) Has this been heard by thee, Pârtha, with an attentive mind? Has the delusion of thy ignorance been destroyed, O Dhananjaya?

Arjuna said:
73) Destroyed is my delusion, and I have gained my memory through Thy grace, O Achyuta. I am firm; my doubts are gone. I will do Thy word.

Sanjaya said:

74) Thus have I heard this wonderful dialogue between Vâsudeva and the high-souled Pârtha, causing my hair to stand on end.

75) Through the grace of Vyâsa have I heard this supreme and most profound Yoga, direct from Krishna, the Lord of Yoga, Himself declaring it.

76) O King, as I remember and remember this wonderful and holy dialogue between Keshava and Arjuna, I rejoice again and again.

77) And as I remember and remember that most wonderful Form of Hari, great is my wonder, O King; and I rejoice again and again.

78) Wherever is Krishna, the Lord of Yoga, wherever is Pârtha, the wielder of the bow, there are prosperity, victory, expansion, and sound policy: such is my conviction.

www.ingramcontent.com/pod-product-compliance
Lightning Source LLC
Chambersburg PA
CBHW030524100426
42813CB00001B/137